FatherEffects

FatherEffects

How your father influenced
who you are and
who you love

Shari R. Jonas, B.A., F.L.E.

Abbeyfield Publishers
Toronto, Canada 2002

Published in 2002 by Abbeyfield Publishers,
a division of The Abbeyfield Companies Ltd.,
33 Springbank Avenue, Toronto, Ontario Canada M1N 1G2
< abbeyfld@istar.ca >

Ordering information:
Distributed in Canada by Hushion House Publishing Ltd.
36 Northline Road, Toronto, Ontario Canada M4B 3E2
Phone (416) 285-6100, Fax (416) 285-1777

National Library of Canada Cataloguing in Publication Data
Jonas, Shari R., 1964–
    FatherEffects: how your father has influenced who you are and who you love

ISBN 1-894584-10-4
1. Mate selection. 2. Fathers and daughters. 3. Man-woman relationships.
I. Title. II. Title: Father effects.
HQ756.J66 2001   646.7'7   C2001-902014-7

Book design: Karen Petherick, Markham, Ontario
Editing: Bill Belfontaine, Abbeyfield Consultants, Toronto, Ontario
Web designer: Harvey Canter: www3.sympatico.ca/hcanter

Cover Photo: Digital Imagery® 1999, Photodisk, Inc.
Printed and bound in Canada

To contact Shari R. Jonas: E-mail: fathereffects@hotmail.com

I dedicate this book:

To my children, Blake Alexander and Andie Cara, who have been
my greatest motivators, teachers and spiritual guides.
Through you, I continually learn what is most important
and most precious.

— *and* —

To every woman who shared her story with me and
every other who has an untold experience;
Always remember that we are stronger and wiser
for the path we have walked on.
We must never question why, but rather, what next.
We are not simply survivors of our experiences,
but warriors of our lives.
We can battle any fear, any setback, any storm.
Let us not be defeated by others who might hurt us
along the way, but challenged by the gift of their lessons.
Strive to live each day in pursuit of happiness.
Allow no one or nothing to get in your way.

In Memory Of

Alexis Crelinsten
Whose beautiful spirit will remain in our hearts and minds forever

Contents

Acknowledgments

A heartfelt thank you to:

Errol Toderovitz – For your incredible listening skills, which enabled me to read every word out loud to you; for your positive reinforcements and constant reminders to write whenever possible, for allowing me to accomplish this project, by giving so much and taking so little. But, most of all, thank you for believing in me, even when I didn't.

My Father, Earle Jonas – For your unconditional support during my choices and crisis, for letting me express myself to you, even when it was difficult to listen, for teaching me the true meaning of, "to err is human", and most of all, thank you for making up for lost time.

Bill Belfontaine – For your editorial wisdom, your professionalism and your patience. But most of all, thank you for showing me that you're never too wise to learn something new.

Karen Petherick – For your phenomenal "intuitive design" as well as, your warmth, guidance and wonderful temperament. Most of all, thank you for appreciating this topic and seeing its merit, as much as I.

Paul Pedullo – For always being just an email away, for never saying, "I can't", for doing so much and never asking for anything in return.

Christopher Benson – My Statistician, whose patience, commitment and knowledge went far beyond the call of duty. May your career in statistics be as unwavering as the dedication you've demonstrated.

Harvey and Agnes Canter – For your constant presence in my life and in my work, for Harvey's website talent and unique ability to walk me through any problem on the computer, while being hundreds of miles away. Most of all, to both of you, for your kindness, acceptance and superb friendship.

Harry Perlman – For steering me in this direction, for helping me to organize my thoughts on paper, for believing in my writing ability, and most of all, for being my greatest fan.

Kimberly Meek, Lisa Lallouz-Ezerzer and my sister, Gianna Wolfe – For opening yourselves up to me and trusting me with your personal histories; for your incredible support, timely words of wisdom, listening ears and most of all, your warm hearts.

Marcy Ellen and Marion Itzikowitz – Two special friends who are too special not to mention. Your presence in my life is filled with love and appreciation.

My older brother Mitchell, my cousin Donna Skolnick and my dear friend Rona Lang – For your presence in my life, I am grateful to each of you for the love and support I have always felt.

Randee Rosenthal Glassman – For the 25 years you've stood by me, for all the joys and heartaches you've shared with me, for your truthfulness, compassion and unwavering friendship, I love you and I thank you.

My Mother, Linda Vosko – For never giving me a difficult time about this subject matter, for accepting my unconventional decisions, for always being a phone call away, for sharing so many dinners with me, for your constant "open door" and most of all, for loving me — no matter what.

My younger brother, Gary Jonas – For understanding the trials and tribulations of getting projects off the ground. For your big heart, deep compassion and amazing generosity. But most of all, thank you for turning roadblocks into stepping-stones.

Gratitude of such magnitude cannot find its place in words, even for a writer.

Affirmation

I believe the sun should never set upon an argument
I believe we place our happiness in other people's hands
I believe that junk food tastes so good because it's bad for you
I believe your parents did the best job they knew how to do.

— Savage Garden

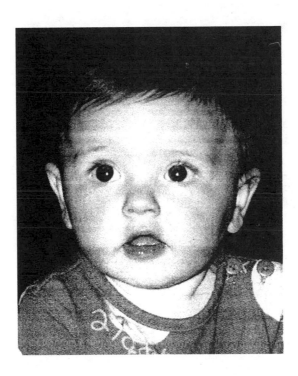

Prologue

Find the seed at the bottom of your heart
and bring forth a flower
— Shigenori Kameoka

Several summers ago, I earned some well-deserved time. It was my calm after a very personal storm, and I knew just what it was I wanted to do; something that I've always thought about. While some people dream of skydiving and others wish to ski the Alps, all I wanted was to plant a flower and vegetable garden — from scratch.

Before I lifted a shovel, or even purchased a pair of sturdy, green, gardening gloves, I researched as much as I could. My plan was to grow beautiful flowers with vibrant colors and cultivate delicious homegrown veggies. I could hardly wait. Yet, the more I read, the more I learned that to achieve the best results, one must concentrate on the soil. The earth must be clear of debris and weeds, while bursting with nutrients. I spent weeks preparing, perfecting and enriching the soil. When there wasn't anything more I could do, I began to plant.

Within two months, I had stunning results. Flowers too beautiful for words, vegetables too scrumptious (and too abundant) to imagine. But, there was nothing more rewarding than the lessons I had learned from the experience. I had taken on this project with the intention to succeed. My heart and soul went into every painstaking step. And I saw incredible results.

With this personal accomplishment, I understood for the first time in my life that what you see on the outside has so much to do with what lies beneath. We are the flowers. Our roots are our history. Our soil is our feelings. Like the garden, it is imperative that you keep your earth healthy, weed out self–deprecating thoughts and clear away destructive behaviors. You must do what it takes to enrich your own soil with nourishing beliefs, positive actions and a healthy attitude. If you do this you will give yourself the opportunity to thrive like never before. And this book can assist you in that process.

There are chapters that will draw you back to your childhood. They will encourage you to examine the relationship you had with your father. Old feelings that you have buried away will resurface. Allow your memories to emerge. Don't be afraid; you are the person you have become today because of those experiences. Satisfied or not by the results, you are unique and so, by definition, you are exceptional.

I can understand your concerns. It may have been some time since you've thought about your childhood, your parents, (particularly your father) and all that transpired. Maybe, you haven't wanted to. But, you are holding this book in your hands, either by choice or by gentle force. If you don't know it already, the reason why you are reading it will come to you in time, if you allow it to.

In my opinion, many people putter around their homes, much the same way they meander through their time on earth. But there comes a moment in everyone's life when we're given the opportunity to stop the nonsense. By reading this book you'll realize that time has arrived.

Make yourself comfortable and be prepared to take in what I hope will be the most thought-provoking material you have read in a long while. As you review and re-evaluate your experiences with your father, be open to change. Become a firm believer that for personal growth, one must reflect on personal history.

Read each question carefully that is listed below. Then, think deeply about each response.

- How did your father make you feel when you were young?
- Can you recall several positive memories of you and your father?

- Can you recall several negative memories that you have of your father?
- How has your relationship with him changed since you became an adult?
- How do you feel about your father today?

Let's turn back the clock. Your father was the very first man in your life. Maybe, not in the literal sense because he might not have been there for you in the physical or emotional way that a parent should be. But, absent or present, your father played a significant part in your childhood. He has impacted upon your personality and influenced your love relationships. Over time, you will realize this, if you haven't already.

Begin by asking yourself if any of your boyfriends, male friends, lovers or husbands remind you of your father or of the relationship you had with your father. If so, this was not a coincidence. In fact, I wouldn't be surprised if you've been in a relationship with someone whose characteristics (physical, behavioral, intellectual or emotional) were completely contrary to his. This was no accident, either. Purposefully, you have been attracting or repelling men that reminded you of your father. Think about that statement. Don't shake your head too quickly. Don't be too eager to disagree.

As you read this book and the stories contained within it, you will begin to understand how your relationship with your father has affected the choices you made regarding the selection of men in your life. Could it be that becoming emotionally involved with someone who reminded you of your father was an attempt to heal old wounds? Perhaps you chose a man who was very different from your father because you didn't want to be treated like your mother. Nor would you ever want to relive your childhood or expose your children to such a man. Do you feel anger or resentment towards your father? Have you ever been able to forgive him? Remember the old expression, "You can run, but you can't hide?" Running can be so very tiresome; especially when it's in circles.

Numerous studies have proven that girls who did not have loving relationships with their fathers exhibited lower self-confidence and achieved less in school. And that is just the beginning. We take our bag of insecurities wherever we go and into every relationship. Women of all ages can testify to this. Being insecure, feeling inadequate, having low self–esteem, are just a few of the emotional issues that will burden you until you are prepared to deal with the very important "roots" of your childhood.

I urge you to take whatever time is needed to reflect upon how your father made you feel. And, take a good, long look at all the boys and men that you've spent your time with. Who have you loved? Who have you hurt? Who have you tried to change? Who broke your heart? If you take the time to do the homework, you will realize there is a strong connection between your self-perception, your father's influence and the relationships you have had in your life. Consider this process an exercise in personal gardening; cleaning out your weeds, turning over your soil and opening your life to the sunshine of self-discovery.

It's never too late to have a happy childhood
— Tom Robbins

My Story 1

Who among us is an expert on the human experience?
We have only the gift of sharing perceptions that
hopefully can help those on their journey.

— Gary Zukav

Every woman has a story to tell about her father. It would be very strange if I had spent all this time studying the relationships that women had with their fathers without examining my own. Some might think that my story was the impetus behind this research but it was not. In fact, it was the ending of my marriage that made me wonder why I chose a man who was so different than myself with whom to spend my entire life. What was I thinking? The answer remained a mystery.

As time went on, I spoke to many divorced women with unsettled childhood issues, particularly women who had unresolved conflicts with their fathers. I was propelled into this research determined to discover the untold stories behind why women chose certain men and what it all had to do with "Daddy." What were *they* thinking when they made their life choice?

As much as women have been inundated with information about how our mothers have affected us, we're still not satisfied with putting the blame solely on Mom. In all fairness, she is only half of the equation. But, the surface of the father-daughter dynamic has hardly been scratched. For me, this relationship became more of a puzzle than any other family pairing. At least it had been.

My story is as unique as yours. I am the middle child, sandwiched in years between two boys. From our recollection and that of our parents there was no love between our mother and father. They were two very different people whose paths were meant to cross only for a short time. Once their marriage was declared over, my father tried to make a life for himself within the same city. Apparently, he could not.

By the time I was ten years old, my father moved back to his hometown in another country, which was more than five-hundred miles away. Even at such a young age, I knew enough about myself to recognize that my mother wasn't solely responsible for all my character traits — good, bad or otherwise. I had this overwhelming need to discover as much about my genetic make up as possible. It was at that point in my life that I decided to get to know my father, first hand.

I reached out to him and fortunately, he responded. I visited him, spoke to him over the phone and listened to audio cassettes that he mailed to me. Those tapes were unforgettable. He compiled songs that either depicted how he felt or that he simply wanted me to appreciate. I related well to my father and found many of my own characteristics in him. I discovered qualities that I appreciated in my father and others that I had not. I came to understand why he and my mother couldn't work it out as husband and wife. Most importantly, I got to know my father, as an individual and I was able to accept him for who he was (and wasn't).

However, I never fully recovered from feeling a deep sense of loss. Every one of my friends had their dads living with them. My father, on the other hand, had packed up and moved hundreds of miles away. As much as I understood why, I still personalized it.

For years, I struggled with a diminished sense of security, self-worth and self-love. You couldn't tell I was suffering by looking at me or spending time with me. I had a very confident façade. But, my relationships with boyfriends were telltale signs that something was amiss.

Throughout my life, I had been fortunate enough to experience several significant and healthy love relationships. Yet, every one of them ended with me realizing how unfulfilled I had become, so I walked away from all of them. Including my marriage.

SHARI R. JONAS

I didn't need a degree in psychology to see that I had clearly developed a relationship pattern. Not only was I the one to leave the relationship, but I did so when the relationship was only two and a half years old. Was there any connection between those short relationships and the fact that I was two-and-a-half-years-old when my father and mother separated? I tend to think that this was not a coincidence, but more of a subconscious strategy to avoid being hurt again. Rather than being abandoned by someone that I loved, I was the one who did the damage by leaving when I did.

And damage I did. By living in fear of my past repeating itself, I was sabotaging wonderful relationships and hurting good people in the interim. Funny how we put people in jail for breaking the law, but those who break hearts remain unscathed. Or do they? It really is a crime to hurt the ones you love because of deep-rooted issues and past traumatic experiences, especially when the person you are hurting the most is yourself.

This is precisely why we must address this unfinished business with our fathers. It doesn't matter whether he left you to be with his alcohol, his drugs, his work or his new wife; we are all equally affected by the absence of our father's consistent and unconditional love. Every girl whose father abandoned, abused, neglected or berated her carries a burden of sadness that penetrates and prevails every relationship she experiences. I know it, others have written to me about it, and I want to share it with you.

Becoming aware of the significant ways in which your father has affected your self-perception and your relationships is an empowering revelation. Do not minimize the impact that he has had on everything important in your life. Rather, choose to maximize it. Take this experience and use it to rise to the occasion. Make it work for you. Learn what *not* to do as a parent. Excel as a partner in *your* relationship. Become more compassionate to the people whose lives you touch. Develop your inner strength to carry you through any storm. And then, inspire others to do the same.

2 | Looking Back

Better by far you should forget and smile,
Than you should remember and be sad.
— Christina Georgina Rossetti

"What the heck were you thinking?" asked my friends after I told them that my marriage was over, rather an odd question to pose under such circumstances. Yet, there was a good reason behind this one. My ex-husband and I were so different. Our personalities supported the time-worn phrase that opposites attract. Anyone that knew us individually could not comprehend what drew us together in the first place. In the beginning, I rationalized our differences, then overlooked them in light of certain character traits which he possessed. Traits, which I thought were more important than common interests, such as working out together or eating the same types of food. Unfortunately, we were so opposite that over time we began to repel one another.

With much reflection, I made an insightful, personal revelation. I wasn't thinking properly when I made the decision to get married. There were too many emotional issues pulling at my heartstrings. Of paramount importance to my state of happiness was my unyielding desire to avoid making the same mistake my parents made. I must have said it a thousand times; *I will never be divorced.*

What I have since learned is that whatever you focus on, positive or negative, will eventually occur. Your subconscious mind works that

SHARI R. JONAS

way; the more you think about something not occurring, the greater the chances that it will.

In my case, I was so driven to not make my parents' mistakes that I made my own and I wound up divorced, in spite of them. In fact, those traits that most attracted me to my ex-husband were non-existent in my father. I married a man who was opposite to my father and I did this to avoid the pitfalls of my parent's doomed marriage. Yet, in making one of life's most crucial decisions, I failed to consider who I was and my personal needs. I really, truly wasn't thinking.

The decision to end my marriage was a major turning point in my life. It provided me with the opportunity to reconcile with my true self and come face-to-face with a myriad of fears and insecurities. For the first time in thirty-three years, I was alone. Alone, except for my three-year-old son, whose happiness motivated me to discover the truth behind my relationship patterns and my unresolved issues. My mission became one of achieving a deeper self-awareness and I began this process by examining my history.

Many believe that one's history begins well before they are born. I learned this from a well–respected and successful family therapist who was teaching a course that I had registered for during this introspective time in my life. It was common practice for this therapist to have her clients, as well as the students in her class, reconstruct their genealogies; so they could study their family tree. The purpose was to educate yourself on your family's physical, emotional and behavioral history. It turned out to be an interesting and educational project. And it wasn't easy. I had to call up and interrogate family members, asking them emotional, personal and thought-provoking questions. "At what age did our relatives die, how did they die, how many siblings did each have, how many marriages, divorces, disasters, disorders, children?" You name it, the questions were asked.

In her professional opinion, this therapist believed that what transpired before you were born was a strong indicator of what patterns you might repeat during your lifetime. Medical doctors ask about your family's medical history, because of the genetic components that are passed on from generation to generation. Who in your family had heart disease, blood disorders, mental illnesses and so on? If the life span of your relatives can predict your life expectancy, isn't it possible that your family's behavioral trends might influence you in a similar fashion?

What was most empowering about completing my family tree was knowing that I had the power to grow my own branches. I could break any behavioral cycle *if* put my mind to it. Just as someone with a family history of heart failure can eat healthier and exercise to alter their genetic prognosis, I could work on improving myself and my future relationships and change my family's unhealthy life patterns. For instance, in my genealogy, there is a high rate of marital discord. In the last generation alone, I witnessed dozens of divorces. My experience with successful marriages is obviously quite limited in scope. Growing up, I became more familiar with marriages dissolving than marriages evolving. Although that doesn't directly explain the reasons for my divorce, it certainly offered me insight as to why my decision to divorce was easier and more acceptable than seeking out other solutions. Broken relationships were all around me, it was what I knew. Yet I still wasn't satisfied.

With the predominance of divorce in our society today and not all family trees resembling my own, I wondered how many women were making soulmate decisions because of past experiences and previous relationships? More importantly, which past relationships were affecting us the most?

I believe that many of us make poor choices because we fail to formulate the distinction between what we know and what we need. What we know is what existed for our parents. If their marriage was strong, we want to emulate it. If it was weak or had failed, we want to avoid repetition.

What we know is the type of men our fathers were. How they treated us, how they treated our mother. If they loved us, we want to find that love. If they were mean, controlling, irresponsible or unavailable, we either attract similar types of men or seek out the complete opposite.

What we need is someone with a special blend of traits that compliment our own. What we need is to focus on our unique person-alities, our individual preferences and our deepest desires. It's so simple and yet, so many of us are fixated on either steering clear of certain types of men, filling "daddy" voids or perpetuating unhealthy relationships, because we just want to make it right. Growing up with a certain type of father or a particular father-daughter relationship appears to have long-term effects. Many of us can attest to that. What I wanted to know was how that experience played itself out in our mate selection.

Having been educated in a research-driven university, I was both familiar and comfortable with the idea of writing up a study. I read all the available books that I could find on fathers and daughters and formulated a one-hundred adjective, multiple-choice questionnaire. Willing participants would select the adjectives which best described themselves, their father, their present significant other, their most compatible significant other, their most difficult significant other and finally, their ideal mate. I posted the first questionnaire on the Internet and was delighted to receive more than 1,000 responses!

By the time I was ready to remove the questionnaire from my website, I had created a second, more detailed survey. This time, the questions were more personal and open-ended. I didn't expect to receive the same number of results as the first questionnaire. It takes a certain type of individual who is willing to candidly share her father-daughter experience with a perfect stranger.

The questions I asked required each participant to recall memories of her childhood, both positive and negative. Often times, I received detailed, emotional responses that evoked a heart-wrenching reaction in me. I am grateful to all 500 participants for their willingness and truthfulness.

And that is how this book came to life: my personal experience, motivated by curiosity, driven by a desire to share these findings with you. Read, enjoy and remember: To all the young women who have not chosen life partners, think first about yourself, your needs and your wants. To all those who have already made a "bad" choice, resolve to examine what drew you to that person. Let us learn from our mistakes and pass these life lessons on to our children, our friends, our neighbors, to anyone who wants to ask, "What the heck were you thinking?"

3 | The Little Girl Inside

When you feel like hope is gone, look inside you and be strong,
because you'll finally see the truth, that a hero lies in you.

— Mariah Carey

Andrea: 44 years old
All the men that I married or wanted to marry were just like my
father. They've all had to be taken care of in some way because
their parents abandoned them and they have a lot of unresolved
feelings. My husband is so much like my father that I want a
divorce. I don't want the kind of marriage my parents had.
Thinking about my father makes me sad because I really miss
him and needed him to be there. I wish he could have talked to
me without becoming so angry. "Daddy, I need to know that you
love me. I've tried to reach out to you and let you know that I love
you. I am hurting. All I want now is to heal the little girl inside
who never felt important to you. Part of my healing means that
I need you to be here for me, but you are not."

When was the last time you had a really good cry? If it wasn't so long ago, then remember how it felt. Was not the depth of your sadness or the fury of your frustration so unbearable that you buried your head in your hands and cried just like a little girl? That's exactly how it felt for me. Oh, women can be so emotional.

Although, not all women are created equal. Some have a more difficult time expressing their pain than others. Why would that be?

When we were young children, we were all uninhibited. Crying, laughing and farting were never taboo — until one day when someone told us to clam up (no pun intended). The expression of our emotions had to be properly timed. You couldn't laugh out loud in the classroom or cry in front of the neighborhood bully. In fact, in my house, I had to pay special attention to the tone in my voice. If I sounded too sarcastic or too disrespectful, I was punished. Needless to say, we've all had to learn how to tame our emotions. The stage at which this restriction kicked in probably occurred between the ages of five and eleven. Preschoolers are not well versed at keeping their emotions to themselves. Yet, pre-teens have got this masking technique down to a science.

These are tender years for a young girl. Maturation comes so quickly it almost sweeps her off her feet. She is emotionally unprepared for the physiological and social challenges that will confront her. Before you know it, that little girl is trapped within a blossoming woman's body. I believe that deep within the psyche of every single woman, there is still a precious, little girl. And when we cry, it is she who is crying. When we feel pain, it is often hers that we are feeling. Intuitively, we all know she exists.

We don't often think of our little girl inside or recall her stories daily, but her spirit remains in our hearts and her memories linger deep within our minds. Many of us would rather not hear her sweet voice again for the recollections could be quite painful, filled with disappointment and despondency. Others might reflect on her often as she brings a smile to their faces when least expected. My late grandmother would often tell me stories of her "little girl's life" in the olden days and whenever she began to recollect, her eyes would gently close. I always imagined that her eyelids were her movie screens and she spoke as if she were reviewing and reliving every moment. How I wished I could have seen what she was seeing or feel what she was feeling. Her little girl was speaking to me and in every instance she had captured my attention. For it was one little girl speaking — almost whispering to another — and nothing is more captivating than a little girl telling a secret.

When was the last time you communicated with a young child? It might have been your niece at the last family gathering or your neighbor's child who lives close by. Possibly, it was with your very own. Whether you address the little girl inside of you or keep her tucked away in the recesses of your mind, interacting with other children always bring her memories to light. It's especially hard to ignore her when Fisher Price, Mattel and Barbie are still manufacturing the same toys today that she used to play with.

To truly interact with a child is to bring out the little girl in yourself. Spending time with a young child reminds us of own buried innocence, curiosity and imagination. Do you ever notice the ease at which a child can bring joy and laughter to a moment? Or, just how quickly the tears can well up in their eyes and pour down their rounded little cheeks when their tender feelings are hurt?

However, being in the company of a child can also bring back the saddest feelings of loneliness and despair. Was it not the little girl inside of you who suffered most, who was robbed of her sense of security, warmth and unconditional love? Recall the very first time you felt utter disappointment. How young were you?

I was nine years old, sitting at the top of the stairs, waiting for my Daddy to come and pick me up. He wasn't just taking me out for dinner. No. Tonight was a special night. He promised to buy me a brand new winter coat. I knew the exact color and style I wanted. My mother (who knew better than I) didn't believe he was going to buy it for me, because he rarely took on those responsibilities. But tonight I was certain, for he solemnly promised the week before — and why would my Daddy lie?

When the doorbell rang, I could hardly contain myself. It didn't bother me that I had been sitting and waiting at the top of the stairs for so long. It was going to be worth it once I had that beautiful, warm winter coat to wear to school the very next day. I rushed down the stairs to greet him and when the door was just about to close behind me, my mother called from the top of the stairs, "Don't forget to buy Shari's winter coat!" My father managed to stop the door from closing long enough to yell back, "Can't do it tonight. I'm a little short for money. But, by next week I should be okay." I never got the coat.

Every woman has a little girl inside. She has the scars of all her childhood pains and every day, in some way, we nurse her wounds. We do this in various ways. We bring people into our lives, we drive them away, we read, we get angry or we cry for the slightest reason. The least effective method is the boys and men we invite into our lives, hoping that they will make our little girl happy, loved and secure, again. They might help for a while, but they will never heal her in the long haul. In truth, there isn't anyone that can mend her broken heart or shattered dreams better than herself.

So, bring forth your little girl. I know she's there, somewhere deep inside of you. Even if you are all grown up, put aside your ego, your façade, your corporate image, whatever walls you've built around her. It is time for you, to reach out and nurture her.

Let Her Recall

*A time when you thought something you did would
surely please someone, but it didn't?
Waiting for someone who never showed?
Feeling alone, even though you weren't?
Wishing for something that you never got?
Pretending someone else was your parent,
instead of the one you had?
Feeling unloved?
A broken promise?
Wanting to run away,
just to see if someone would notice?
A situation that caused someone to become so angry
and you didn't know why?
Caring for your favorite doll the way you wished
someone would care for you?
Being interrupted by screaming and fighting,
from just outside your bedroom door?
The fear that pervaded every little bone in your body
when you heard footsteps approaching your room?
Crying in your pillow, but no one caring?*

The past will never change. But, with love and attention — we can make a difference in our future. Begin by healing old and deep wounds. Cry for the little girl inside of you. Mourn for her losses, honor her pain, talk about her fears and love her with all your adult heart. She is a very big part of who you are today and together you can develop the inner strength to battle your demons and conquer your enemies.

What are some of your deepest scars? Here's a hint; your adult relationships with men are tell-tale signs of how you were treated as a child. Are you always treated with respect? Do you give more to a man than you get in return? Have you ever accepted inappropriate or abusive behavior? Are you sacrificing yourself or your children in any way? Do you wish to leave, but feel you cannot? Do you wish for more, but do not receive it?

The relationship you had with your father can offer you tremendous insights as to why you behave the way that you do and tolerate as much as you have. What I always found interesting about human behavior is that often times we know better — but we don't do better. The reason for this is a combination of fear and habit. We're afraid to do something different, after having done the same thing for so long. We're all creatures of habit who fear the unknown. It's a form of mental paralysis. Yet, we must keep in the forefront of our minds that we are free. Free to change our lives, change our situation, change the way we allow people to treat us. We must learn how and then begin the process.

Since many of us cannot go back and discuss with our fathers or mothers what truly happened and why, we have only to ask ourselves. To do this, we must address the little girl who resides within us. Honoring her is both significant and paramount to your overall well-being. She is inundated with secrets that contain the pains and pleasure of your childhood. If you just ask her, she can answer many questions as to who you are and how you came to be. Listen carefully. When it comes to understanding your relationship with your father, she has a wealth of information. She was there, ever present, and she lives deep within you — awaiting your permission to come forth and be loved.

If you are truly prepared to nurture the little girl inside of you, there are three approaches I can suggest. Select the one that best suits your personality or alternate amongst them.

Journaling: This exercise has become quite popular over the years and rightfully so. It is a highly effective method of clearing out cobwebs and confronting personal issues. You don't have to be a writer to jot down a feeling. You just need the time and the tools (pen and paper). It's amazing how the words will flow from you like an undammed river.

Meditating: Sit peacefully in a quiet place. In this instance, imagine yourself sitting in front of your little girl. Listen for her thoughts or simply see yourself holding her hand. Feel yourself comforting her. Be receptive to her. But, most important, be patient with her. It has been a very long time since you've connected.

Collaging: Collect pictures of yourself from infancy to adolescence. Either mount them onto a large piece of cardboard or place them in an album. Play music in the background during this time. Don't allow yourself to think. Rummage through old pictures and select the ones that elicit an emotion, placing them wherever your intuition guides you.

With each task ask your little girl's assistance. Listen for that inner voice for it is hers, guiding you, enlightening you and stimulating your senses. Allow the thoughts, images, and feelings to play themselves out in your mind. Feel her pain, empathize with her sadness, rejoice in her delight. And write about it. Or meditate on it. Or create a collage to express it. This project could take a day, a week or even longer. You'll know when it's done, when the little girl inside you tells you so. Just listen.

Charlene. 40 years old

I remember my father rocking me as a baby and the peace I felt when he held me. He always smelled of cigar smoke. At first, I thought I wanted someone who resembled my father's characteristics; the strong and silent type. Then I went the other way and chose someone who was exactly opposite both physically and emotionally. I was wrong in both cases. I see now that I never chose someone for myself, but for resemblance or non-resemblance to my father.

First Love | 4

If you find it in your heart to care for somebody else,
you will have succeeded.

— Maya Angelou

Alison, 24 years old

My parents divorced when I was six years old. After that, I only saw my father on the weekends. Eventually, he stopped calling and stopped showing up. I haven't seen nor heard from my dad since 1988, when he was put into prison. I have always been very unsure of my father's love for me. Whenever I meet someone who reminds me of my dad, I refuse to have anything to do with him. My relationship with my father has made me feel uncertain about all male relationships. In fact, most of my life decisions have been based on the notion that anything could change drastically from one moment to the next. Just like my father did with me, I have the ability to drop a relationship and all contact with that person. I can honestly say that I have never felt as if anyone ever cared about me. If I could quit crying long enough to talk, I would tell my father that I love him today, just as I always have. I often wonder why he had me in the first place if he never wanted me. Still, I have always been willing to forgive my father for his absence. How I wish things could have been different for us. All I ever wanted was my father to be there for me. I feel so empty and sad inside. I am so insecure. I lost out on one of life's most important treasures; a relationship with my dad.

Can you remember the first boy who you fell in love with? Close your eyes and think about him, for just a minute. What was his name? How old were you? Where were you when you first looked into each other's eyes and held each other's hand? Now, don't go thinking about how it ended. Just, remember how it felt to be with him. When you were together, time stood still. Even when you were amongst a group of friends, you felt special because he was there. The very thought of him was exhilarating. You felt alive. What a wonderful feeling.

I'll never forget the first boy I fell in love with. It was the summer that I turned thirteen. I was coasting along on my skateboard with my best friend Randee close by on hers. That's when I saw him. He was on his bicycle when our paths literally crossed. I don't know what made us all stop, but we did. It turned out that David didn't live very far away and he soon developed the habit of bicycling down my street, hoping to find me hanging outside my house or skateboarding around our neighborhood.

David was turning sixteen at the end of that summer. It didn't bother me that he was more mature than any boy I ever liked. I was more concerned with how my older brother would handle it, since they were the same age. Throughout that summer, David and I spent many days together. We talked for hours. He was different from most boys I knew. He was confident and knew how to handle himself around a girl. But, what stands out most in my mind was the way he made me feel when put he arms around me. I remember that feeling as if it happened yesterday. I was so young and yet, so very much in love. Although David might have been the first boy I ever loved, he was not the first man.

Think back to the first man that you fell in love with. Remember the first time he held you in his big, strong arms? His kisses were so soft and his touch was so gentle. The warmth of his body against yours was very comforting. Sleep came easier when you felt so secure, so loved. Can you remember? It was so long ago . . . .

SHARI R. JONAS

Let me answer this one for you. You can't possibly remember how you felt because — you were just a baby. The first man you've ever loved was none other than your father.

Imagine yourself as an infant. You came into this world needing warmth, nutrition and love. Unless your father was absent the moment before you exited the womb, his arms were the first male arms that were wrapped around your little body. This was your first tactile experience with the opposite sex and though you were just an infant, the bond between you and your father began to develop. This is a natural and reciprocal phenomenon. Not only are babies genetically programmed to initiate bonding immediately following their birth, researchers have found that within the first few days of an infant's life, fathers actually become *hooked* on their infants.

I have seen this magic with my daughter and her daddy. She was born by emergency caesarian section. It was a last minute decision and I wasn't emotionally prepared. For anyone who has not experienced a caesarian, it is a real operation; bright lights, sterile gowns and a real chill in the air. Fear, rather than excitement, filled my every thought. Within minutes, they pulled her out of me, but I could barely see her. If it weren't for her set of lungs, I would never have known that she was in the room.

While they sewed me up, I focused my attention on the bond that was forming right before my eyes. After she was weighed, examined and bundled the nurse placed her in her father's arms. I watched his face as he held our precious daughter. He seemed to love her more with each passing moment. For hours, she remained perfectly content in the warmth and security of her daddy's arms. That was the very first day of her life and I was convinced that she felt connected to her daddy immediately.

Unfortunately, not all baby girls have had the same tangible opportunity. There are many who were given up for adoption and oodles more whose fathers never claimed them as their own. Yet, why is it that these girls who have never known their fathers still feel hurt, rejected and abandoned? Why do they continually search for the love that their fathers never gave them in the arms of other men? The answer is simple. Whether you knew your father or not, the need to be loved by him is a deep, emotional need that is rooted in our biological and psychological make up. We feel connected to our fathers because they co-created us. We are a part of them. Shouldn't they love us just because of that?

For many women, their father's love was their first love. For others, it was their first disappointment.

If your father was unable or unwilling to provide you with unconditional love, even if he was abusive, all is not lost. You needn't worry that your eternal happiness rests on your father's merits or on his faults. It absolutely doesn't. Your happiness and the success of your relationships depends solely upon *you*. You have only to realize that the misdirected or idle love you have for your father needn't be wasted on men less deserving.

From this day onward, turn that love inward and nurture your little girl. She's been hurting long enough. And when the healing is complete, consider sending that immense amount of love outward to those who will greatly appreciate it: your children, your pets, even your favorite charity.

Beth, 28 years old

I definitely look for the love that I didn't feel from my father. Consequently, I don't assess people enough to see whether I really like them. I just dive into the relationship. What I look for is a person who is capable, intellectual and interesting, someone I could look up to, like my father. That way, if they love me then it means that my father did too. Right? My father died of cancer when I was twenty-one years old. We got a bit closer when he was dying, perhaps because he lost his speech and we couldn't fight! Although we had a difficult relationship, I felt we had some resolution. Although I'll never know for sure if he ever loved me.

SHARI R. JONAS

When the
Bubble Bursts

*Our real blessings often appear to us in the shapes of pains,
losses and disappointments; but let us have patience, and
we soon shall see them in their proper figures.*
— Joseph Addison

Cindy, 27 years old
*The best word to describe my father would be "gone." He has
slowly moved out of our lives. After my parents divorced, we had
the occasional weekend visit, but no strings attached. When I
was thirteen, my father remarried a woman from a wealthy
family. But, in order to do so, he had to hide the fact that he was
previously married and therefore, had to hide his children. There
were no signs of us in his house, no pictures, cards we sent,
nothing. In essence, we were no longer a part of his everyday life.
We were more like ghosts from the past that occasionally come
back to haunt him. To describe my father during those years of
my life — irresponsible, selfish and full of broken promises. At
about age fourteen, I was in counselling for my rebellious
attitude. My father was required to come to one session in a safe
place so that I could say how much I needed him. He made his
promises that things were going to be different. He was full of
hugs and kisses. Weeks later, everything was the same.*

*I desperately craved my father's approval; anything to get
him to be proud of me. I guess I felt that I wasn't good enough
if he had to hide the fact that I was alive. When I would spend
a weekend with him, he would tell me that I was his favorite girl
and I wanted so badly to believe this.*

To seek my father's approval, you name it — I tried it. I tried all the sports and pushed myself to do the best. I tried excelling in school and being the perfect daughter. Then I gave up at about age fifteen. I completely rebelled, screaming for attention. Unfortunately, he didn't pay attention to that either.

My husband isn't anything like my father, as far as emotions and personality. He is open, he believes in discussing everything and he offers words of encouragement before I have to ask for them. My most difficult relationship was with someone who was just bad all around. I ended it when I found out that I was pregnant and didn't want my child to grow up with a man like that. As a result of my relationship with my father, I'm afraid that I always crave attention from men. Even now, after I'm married.

What I loved most about my father was that he was my daddy and a little girl always loves her daddy. Somewhere along the way, I created this fantasy in my mind of a father/daughter relationship. But my father was never what a daddy should be. Whenever he wasn't around, I would pretend that the next time I would see him, he would fit that image. I still love him because he is my father and somewhere inside of him, maybe, just maybe, that man that I dreamed of as a little girl is there. I just have to wait for him to come out.

"Dad, all I ever wanted was for you to love me and for you to take pride and joy in my accomplishments. I miss you terribly. I forgive you for all the things in the past."

The Father-Daughter Fantasy

The best definition of the word 'fantasy' can be found in *Webster's Seventh New Collegiate Dictionary*. *Fantasy: the free play of creative imagination.* It doesn't only sound healthy, but it connotes innocence and youthfulness. As a young girl, I would fantasize about many things. I was a beautiful lady in my mom's high-heeled shoes. I was a world famous chef with my Easy Bake oven. I was a high-powered executive

S H A R I   R.   J O N A S

with my manual typewriter. I was the doting mother to twenty-five dolls — none of which kept me up all night. The list goes on and on.

Childhood fantasies are quite common. They can be simple and straightforward or complex and convoluted. Many are fleeting, while others are played out for years. However, there is one fantasy in particular, that often develops in the mind of a little girl, which is more meaningful, more hopeful and ultimately, more painful to let go. That is the fantasy between her and her daddy.

This one is not a very elaborate fantasy, as far as details and imagination go. You simply are Daddy's Little Girl. You and he share a very special bond, a secret code that no one can break. The way he looks at you, talks to you and includes you in his plans, when you know he doesn't have to. When you're with your daddy, it's as if time stands still. At least, you wished it would.

For many girls, this was not their fantasy, but their reality. The relationship they shared with their father was a positive and empowering experience. The memories they have will be treasured for a lifetime. Events, occasions and moments are so unforgettable that these girls spend years reminiscing about their fathers. Every time they retell a story, it's more exciting, more wondrous than ever before. "Could you believe MY father did that for me?" Sentences that begin with, "My dad and I," resonate with pride and adoration. He's become a legend in her mind. Is it any wonder that she always wanted to marry someone — just like him?

But, for so many girls whose relationships with their fathers ranged from non-existent to cruel and unthinkable, their creative imagination was their only salvation. Pretending that your daddy was a king and you were his princess was a temporary reprieve from the emotional turmoil that wreaked havoc on your heart.

It might not have felt so bad to have a daddy who mistreated you or made you feel insignificant, if it weren't for all the others. Your best friend, your neighbor and your cousin seemed to have the perfect father. It made you wonder what you did to deserve a dad like yours. Fortunately, you were able to rely on your imagination to allow you to escape your unjust reality

But, it was only a matter of time. The day would surely come when your bubble would burst. It's an predictable certainty, a guaranteed occurrence and a profound revelation that would change you for the rest of your life. The moment that you realized the truth about your father, all your fantasies of him and your imaginary relationship would come to a crashing halt. Even the best of daddies can deflate into mere mortals.

The two most common catalysts for this inevitable time bomb is adolescence and divorce. When Mom and Dad break the news to the family that their marriage is failing, generally it's your father who moves out. If you had any illusions about your relationship with him while he was living with you, the test of all time comes when he's living on his own. Often times, visitations become infrequent, promises become broken and support in all areas becomes erratic. What did you expect from a father who demonstrated his love for you primarily in the fantasies that you created and rehearsed in your own mind? Yes, the divorce changed him. But to some degree, he was always that way. You were just too immersed in your illusions to see otherwise. It was only a matter of time.

As for the bubble bursting while adolescence is erupting, this has everything to do with one's autonomy and sexuality. The raging hormones of a teenage girl are the driving force behind her need to blossom and break away. Even the most loving fathers have difficulty with this stage of development. Often, it is he who distances himself from his daughter during these challenging years. Her need to socialize with friends and investigate her womanhood challenges the dynamics of their changing relationship until the dust settles. In many cases and several stormy years later, a new father-daughter relationship is established.

But, for girls whose fantasies of their fathers were just that, the bubble bursting is a life-altering discovery. He is no longer her hero and mentor who could do no wrong, but a man with imperfections and idiosyncrasies. Her rose-colored glasses are replaced with lenses of anger and sadness. This man who calls himself her father is distant and disapproving. She can't get close to him and even when she tries, she is unable to please him. Her self-esteem takes a beating and so does their relationship.

S H A R I   R.   J O N A S

When a young girl's perception of her perfect father changes, she reacts in ways that hurt her the most, although she doesn't know it at the time. She might rebel, do poorly in school, dress outrageously, argue with him incessantly, become promiscuous or even pregnant.

Bursting this bubble is a necessary process in breaking away from your father. It is difficult and upsetting. Yet, it can be overcome. The eyes of a child see what they want to see. The eyes of an adolescent see what they care to see. But the eyes of an adult can see truth and accept it, without judgment and without anger. In breaking free, you realize that you and your father are not one and the same. He is who he is and you are who you are. Be thankful for that.

The question now is where are you today? Are you still angry with your father for how he treated you then? Does the thought of him sadden you or make your stomach turn? Have you allowed your negative feelings to creep into every love relationship you've ever had? Are you plagued with low self-esteem and struggle with trust issues? Have you become a control freak to ensure that no one will ever hurt you like that again? Answering yes to anyone of these questions suggests that you are still burdened with issues. If you think that burying them into the recesses of your mind is the solution, then think again.

To resolve anything, it is necessary to reflect, restructure and reprogram. Reflect on the experience. Restructure your perceptions to see yourself, your father and the events that took place from a different and broader perspective. Finally, reprogram your thoughts. The significant people in your life have crossed your path for a purpose. Dig deep within yourself and find out how you've benefited from the relationship, because you have. In life, it's not what happens to you that will define who you are, but what you make of it. And, it's never too late to start doing the right thing.

The darkest hour is just before dawn.
— Mamas and Papas

Sarah, 31 years old

My father was accused of murder and spent twenty-three years in prison. (He had a drinking problem, which put him in a bar situation, where he ended up meeting the woman he was accused of murdering.) Before he went away, I remember sitting on his lap at the kitchen table, feeling very secure and loved. While he was away he wrote the greatest letters. I knew him as this loving, gentle soul at the other end of a pen. Unfortunately, when he returned, he never contacted me. He went to prison as a good father, maintained that role in his letters and came back clueless as to how to be a father. I reached out to him for love and a relationship, but he wasn't there. I still miss the fact that I will never be a daddy's girl. I feel sad for the loss and I want to curl up and cry. I thought I had come to terms with it, but I guess it will always be in my heart. I love my dad very much and would love to hear from him. I think if I had a relationship with him, it would help to complete me. There are times I wish he had gotten the electric chair. Then, I would have had the memory of my father's letters, when he loved me so much, instead of this strange man who came back home.

Remembering Your Father | 6

Can it be that it was all so simple then
Or has time rewritten every line?
— Barbara Streisand

Human memory has been researched and studied for hundreds of years. Yet, there is still an ongoing debate as to how memory functions.

What are memories made of? According to Professor Danielle Lapp, of Stanford University and author of several books on memory, the answer is rather interesting. "Memories are made of feelings, moods, thoughts and words involving the senses, the emotions, the imagination and the intellect."

Many of us depend heavily on our memories and yet, as we shall see, they may not be as reliable and accurate as we've imagined. Before you refute or deny this possibility, let's review the basic functions of our memory processes.

As we walk through life, we perceive through our senses, an abundance of information, events and experiences. What is selected then becomes stored into either short-term memory or long-term memory. The difference between these two areas is simply that short-term memory is transient and of limited capacity while long-term memory can be endless and permanent. Processing an event, whereby we take it from short-term memory into long-term memory, requires several necessary components. Rehearsal and repetition are the foundation for long-term storage. In the absence of rehearsal, events are more likely to be forgotten. Furthermore, long-term memory relies on intensive observation, analysis and judgment — and judgment, involves emotion. Emotions play a complex and significant role in your memory function. Positive emotions are so powerful that they can effectively seal a memory, protecting it from the ravages of forgetfulness. Studies indicate that what we remember most is what moves and touches our hearts and soul".[1]

Based on memory research, it is easy to understand why certain memories are clear and easy to recall, while others are long forgotten. The day-to-day events that have occurred throughout our life do not get stored in our long-term memory primarily because they are not rehearsed in our mind. Furthermore, they are mundane, trivial and lack the necessary affective elements to have any staying power. On the other hand, when an event occurs that is meaningful, emotional and significant, such as a birthday party in which we received a long-awaited puppy, we recite this experience in our minds and to those around us so often that it becomes embedded in our long-term memory.

The same encoding process takes place with a negative experience. The emotional or physical pain of an event gets played out and retold so often, that it too, becomes a part of our long-term memory. It is true that we are capable of blocking out painful or traumatic events so that we are not immobilized by the psychological effects on a daily basis. This blocking out process does not preclude the experience from entering our long-term memory. It is a psychological method of burying the event into our subconscious, so that we can function on a daily basis. Through hypnosis and psychoanalysis, repressed memories can be brought out, in hopes of understanding and resolving the traumatic experience.

Memory performance is greatly affected by age. Both young children and the elderly share many common factors that explain their difficulties in storing and retrieving memories. Short attention span, lack of awareness, difficulty forming mental pictures, difficulty in

---

1   *(Nearly) Total Recall, A Guide to a Better Memory at Any Age*, Danielle C. Lapp,1992, Stanford, California, Stanford Alumni Association (Publishers),
2   *Eyewitness Testimony*, Elizabeth F. Loftus, 1979, Cambridge, Massachusetts, Harvard University Press (Publishers).

SHARI R. JONAS

focusing and difficulty in selecting important elements are just a few of the cognitive skills that are lacking in children and diminishing in most seniors. Without these basic thought processes the recording of information into long-term memory becomes greatly inhibited.

No matter what age you are, nobody remembers everything. Memory is subjective: each person chooses to remember what interests her or him. According to Lapp[2], our personalities filter and interpret everything we are exposed to. Passively and unconsciously, each person makes a different selection of which elements to retain, for not all memories are of equal importance or intensity. Some memories disappear where others leave a strong mark, while still others bloom and expand because of multiple recalls.

Recent studies suggest that our memories are continually being altered, transformed and even distorted. This happens because every time we remember something, we tamper with that memory, adding to it some present association or weakening another part of it. *Each time you recall an event, you add or leave out part of the original memory.* Memories do not remain intact. Let me repeat that, memories do not remain as intact. Elizabeth Loftus, a specialist in eyewitness testimony, suggests that, "Even if we take in a reasonably accurate picture of some experience, it does not necessarily stay intact in our memory. Another force is at work here. The memory itself, can actually undergo distortion." This explains why people report the same episode differently. According to Loftus, "It's because often, we do not see things as they are."

In her work, Loftus has discovered that eyewitnesses rarely agree on what transpired. They often contradict one another and may even make false accusations. Human beings tend to see what they expect to see and that, in turn, becomes their memory.

From all that you've just read, would it be fair to say that not all our memories are one hundred percent accurate, reliable and consistent over time? Yet, despite the evidence, we tend to hang onto our memories, believing them as factual and allowing them to navigate us through relationship situations and beyond.

How often do you hear yourself say, "I am this way because of a particular experience?" We tend to define ourselves or rationalize our behavior by our memories, which as we have learned, are influenced by our emotions. Can you see now how the memory of any experience or of someone in your past may have been modified or even eroded over time?

Understand that I am not questioning your most painful memories, those that are seared into your long-term memory because of their unacceptable and horrific details. Nor do I expect you to doubt any of the beautiful and positive experiences that you have been so fortunate to have had in your life. I would like you to accept the possibility that much of what we remember from childhood and adolescence is so subjective that it might not be as accurate as we've imagined.

Remember the definition of memories early in this chapter? They're made of feelings, moods, thoughts, words, emotions, imagination and intellect. If, for example, you were not sure whether your father loved you, wouldn't your memories of him be filled experiences to support those uncomfortable thoughts and emotions? Your imagination might have embellished some of your memories over time in order for you to support your own adult insecurities.

Have you ever heard the phrase, "Your perception is your reality?" I understand that what your memories tell you about your past is all that you know. But, I would like you to begin to seriously consider how you've interpreted your past — what you believe to be true in light of the memories that you carry around, memories that you use to define yourself and those that you take with you into your significant relationships.

Keep in mind that much of what we know from childhood is a compilation of other peoples' stories, recollections and memories. I can recall looking at old photographs often enough that I believed the events were actual memories. Possibly, photographs do jog our long term memory banks and link us back to specific events in our life, but often times, those photographs were shown to us with a story attached to it—somebody else's story that, with repetition and conviction, we've come to believe is true.

Who would you be if you could erase every single one of your negative memories? Would you have any sadness, any anger, any insecurity in your life? Over the years, you have developed your own character, though you might have struggled with certain traits that

SHARI R. JONAS

developed as a result of past experiences. By letting go of the negative memories of your past, your true character can emerge and begin to evolve. For underneath your layers of pain and insecurity lies a special person capable of having meaningful, loving relationships. Whether or not this can happen is completely and totally up to you.

Consider the possibility that you use your memories to justify who you are and that type of thinking prohibits you from becoming a different person, perhaps even a happier person? If this is the case, should you continue to allow your negative memories to dictate your life any more than they already have? Is it really beneficial to your character, to your relationships, to your life to lug your disturbing childhood memories around like a heavy ball and chain? If you are a good person, a good friend, a good mother — you are that way now by choice. The goodness in you will not change if you let go of the pain from the past. The time has come to acknowledge, accept and release all your negative childhood memories. Unchain yourself and let those memories remain buried in the past — where they rightfully belong.

Here's an interesting exercise.

Take a large sheet of paper and draw a line down the center, followed by a line across the middle. You should have four equally-divided boxes on the page. In the upper left quadrant, write, "Appealing Qualities." In the box below, please write, "Positive Memories." In the upper right box add, "Unappealing Qualities" and below that, "Negative Memories". Before filling in the four boxes, think long and hard about this exercise.

For the first time in your life, you are going write about your father as if he is a character in a movie that you are working on. List as many appealing and unappealing qualities/traits about your "leading man" in the proper boxes. As you enter a quality, think of a positive or negative statement that can support that character trait and write it in the box alongside. For this, you will have to draw on a particular memory. For example, if you write that your father is a loving man, follow this with a loving memory — an incident or event where he demonstrated "lovingness" to you   written in the appropriate box. On the other hand, if your father is a cold or cruel man, remember an experience you

The Name of Your "Leading Man"

Appealing Qualities	Unappealing Qualities

Positive Memories	Negative Memories

had encountered with him where he demonstrated to you just how cold or cruel he could be. Try to use a minimum of five adjectives to describe him in both the appealing and unappealing categories.

Many of you might find this task difficult. You might not have any positive characteristics to describe your leading man. If this is your dilemma, I would like you to imagine the following scenario. Your father is an old and dear friend. Someone who you know well and accept, despite all his human imperfections — and imperfections he has many. You knew your friend when he was a young boy; you knew his family, his environment and his circumstances. Better than most people, you understand why he is the way he is. In all fairness to your long-time friend and for the purpose of your script (you do want your viewers to see the full scope of your character's nature) write down some of your friend's better character traits.

A second reason you might find this exercise difficult is because your father is such an amazing man, you can't muster up nor support any unappealing qualities. Reality check: Your leading man is not a perfect human specimen. He has faults and flaws just like you and me. Remember, your task is to step outside of your adoring role as his daughter and see all sides of his character; good, bad or otherwise.

A third and final reason you might find this task to be a struggle is because you've never thought of your father as anyone other than your father. Being a parent carries tremendous expectations and with that, the possibility of enormous disappointments. A young child's perspective of their parent is limited and personalized. But, you are an adult now and can go beyond the scope of a child's understanding. A father is not an infallible person. Identify something positive about him. Don't be afraid to rehash your memories and replace them with different ones. You are older now. You see the world from another perspective than when you were younger. See your father differently — if you can. One day you might have a child, (if you aren't a mother already) who might have to do this exercise with you in mind.

Jennifer, 26 years old

I've had many fathers because my mother had been married four times during my adolescence. My mother and biological father got divorced when I was four. They were forced to get married when my mom was sixteen because she had become pregnant with me. After my parents divorced, my father gave up his rights to me so that my new step-dad could adopt me. I have always felt rejected by him — my father. Eventually we moved out of state. My mom told me a lot of bad things about my father, so I became scared of him. I do remember one night when he and my mom were still married, he came home with a dozes roses for her. When she threw them in his face, he beat her until she passed out on the floor. I remember the way he glared at me. I have always blamed myself for my parent's unhappiness.

I remember my father being a quiet, reserved man who never seemed to know what to say to me when I was around. The funny thing is, I have always felt that he loved me even though he never showed it or said it. My dad has this way of saying things without words. He has never told me anything bad about my mom and has never made up any excuses for why he gave me up. The first time he told me that he loved me, he cried. I just know that he loves me. This might not make sense to some people; how can I know something like that if the person never tells you. But, he shows me in other ways. He travelled six hundred miles to see me graduate high school and I had never seen anyone look so proud. He used to send money for birthdays and holidays but that could never replace the time I wish we had spent together.

Like my father, I have a tendency to bottle up my emotions. I rarely let anyone see how I am feeling. Even when I become comfortable with someone, I still keep my wall up to protect myself. I think he was hurt really badly in his life and that he regrets some of the mistakes he's made regarding me. He's missed my entire childhood and I've been hurt by his absence. It seems we both have a hard time trusting people.

Fortunately, I have taken numerous psychology courses at school. I have learned to always be aware of the choices I make and why I make them. My fiancé is very different from my father. He is open about his feelings and would never lay a hand on me. It works because we communicate and trust one another. He is also quite androgynous, while my dad was the epitome of a man.

I hope to never repeat any negative patterns from child-hood. That would be completely self-defeating. "Dad, I love you. I know how hard it was for you and my mom. Please know that I forgive you for whatever you feel you have done wrong to me."

SHARI R. JONAS

Releasing
Your Father

7

What drives my life today is the energy that I generate in
my present moments.

— Dr. Wayne Dyer

I love it when I hear a person say, "I can forgive, but I can never forget." Where is the reality in this statement? Releasing a negative memory is a challenging human task. There's no question. But to forgive someone while holding onto that negative experience is nearly impossible. For as long as you hold on, you never let go. The truth is that we cling to a bad memory because we feel it will protect us from falling victim once again. So, we are choosing to remember. It's our defense. Over time, we define ourselves by the unforgivable and unforgettable acts of other people. "I am this way because my father was this, wasn't that, did this or didn't do that." Who then, decides your fate?

The exercise at the end of the previous chapter was designed to see your father as a human being and attach specific memories to that individual. Let's take a look at one of my memories;

Unappealing quality — Selfish; my father always put himself first.

Supporting memory — He moved to another country because it suited him. He had a whole bunch of reasons, personal and financial, but he certainly wasn't thinking about his children's needs.

As a young girl, I defined myself by the memory of my father's departure. "He left me, therefore I must not be good enough." For years, I struggled with this. Today, I am able to redefine the rationale behind that same memory. I understand that he might have been lonely, financially strapped and desperate to start his life over again. Really, I had nothing to do with my father leaving. In fact there wasn't anything I could have done to make him stay. Personally, it was something he had to do. It's not something I would have done if I were in his shoes. But, I am not here to judge him. We are two separate people with two separate ways of thinking. If my older brother was in the same position, emotionally and financially, I wouldn't agree with him leaving his children, but I would understand.

Attaching specific memories to another person's characteristics gives you an objective viewpoint. In essence, you are releasing yourself from the effects of that person's behavior. You might not agree with how another person operates, but you don't have to take it personally, either.

When my father left the home I was only two and a half years old. My memories of him consisted primarily of telephone conversations, weekly visits and summer vacations. Much of what I had been told about my father came from my mother and then later, by my brothers. My memories of him did not support all that I had been told, for I had very little to go on; certainly not enough to ban him from my life forever. To resolve the conflict in my own mind, I had to spend years getting to know my father for myself, in order to determine the kind of person he really is.

Today, I can clearly see the good and the not-so-good in my father. Furthermore, I can support every one of his appealing and unappealing traits with memories — my memories. He is not a perfect man. He has made some terrible mistakes in his life, mistakes I wish he had never done for he has hurt family members whom I love. But, neither he, nor I, can change what has happened. However, I will not hold him in contempt for the rest of his life or mine. I believe he is paying the price for his mistakes and the remorse that I sense in my father becomes another appealing quality. Maybe, that's just me. For I can see many sides of a person's character and I am a very forgiving (and forgetting) person. It is in my nature to live and let live. My philosophy is that I want people to accept me for all of my human imperfections and in turn, I find it within myself to accept theirs.

Whether you despise your father or adore him, I would like you to approach your father from an objective standpoint. He is a human being whose memories and experiences molded his character well before you came into his life. Many of his personality traits might not be the most ideal, but they are a result of his life circumstances. Unfortunately, you might have had to suffer for all that he went through, but that is something you have to accept. Did you choose him as a father? Did he choose you as a daughter? So, whom then should we blame?

If you really had difficulty with the previous written exercise and could not step back and see your father for his good and bad characteristics, then at least try to see your relationship with your father as an experience, a life lesson. As with all life experiences, there are positive and negative outcomes. Possibly this experience with your father has made you a stronger person, a more sensitive person or simply, a more loving person. Unfortunately, you might have been left with scars; an inability to trust, fear of abandonment, low self esteem or just plain anger. But in order for you to truly benefit from this life lesson, you must see it for all that it has taught you — for all it's worth.

Our bodies grow when we feed it food and water. Our souls evolve when we empower it with the experiences that are presented to us throughout our lifetime. Every pleasurable moment, as with every positive person, is a gift. The same holds true for every negative moment and every nasty individual. If only we could embrace our adversaries as easily as we embrace our allies — for they are, in fact, one and the same; they are all our teachers. All who touch our lives, who bring us joy or sorrow, love or pain, have been sent to us.

However, once the lesson has been learned, we can choose to dismiss those individuals from our lives. We can let them go, just as we can release the negative memories associated with them. This is our choice and there is nobody who can rob us of our inalienable right to chose the people we surround ourselves with. If your father has hurt you, accept him for who he is, learn the lessons he has brought forth to you, become a better person for having had the experience — then release him.

8 | Stories From the Heart

Learn from the mistakes of others,
You can't live long enough to make them all yourself
— Eleanor Roosevelt

I have spent the last three years reading and comparing hundreds of women's stories. I did so because I wanted to understand the impact that fathers had on their daughter's choices. Considering all the choices that women make in their lifetime, I focused on one particular area. Men. What are women thinking about when they spend time with someone of the opposite sex? More specifically, whom are they thinking about? Since Daddy is usually the first male in their life, I wondered whether he consciously or subconsciously, directly or indirectly, influenced their mate selection.

This prompted the second survey comprised of open ended questions which were personal and thought-provoking. Astonishingly 500 women of all ages, managed to dig deep within themselves and unselfishly share their experiences. For reasons of confidentiality, I have changed the name of every woman whose story has been told in my book.

To break down a very complex relationship, I asked the contributors to define their relationships with their fathers based on whether their memories were positive, negative or mixed. It was the easiest question they had to answer. The rest was uphill.

Within one year, I received an array of father/daughter stories that ranged from unconditional love and adoration, to deep-rooted insecurity

SHARI R. JONAS

and disappointment, to impenetrable anger and unfathomable pain. Although each story was different, they all had something in common. There was not a single woman with a difficult, distant or non-existent relationship with her father that wanted it to be that way. Circumstances, far beyond their control, were the driving force. Parents' relationships, fathers' characteristics, life's stressors were paramount amongst the contributing factors.

However, many things can change once a young girl reaches adulthood. What was beyond her control becomes within her reach. She has a handful of choices, where before there were none. The adult daughter, if willing, can modify many aspects of her present-day relationship with her father; including purpose, quality and most importantly, her attitude.

Making these emotional amendments is very therapeutic. If a woman can resolve deep-rooted issues with her father, she need not drag them into every relationship, as so many have done in this study.

Interestingly, the issues and upsets that the women revealed were not as unique and independent from one another. There was plenty of overlap and repetition: alcoholic fathers who sexually abused their daughters or emotionally unavailable men who thought nothing of beating up their children. As a result of this second questionnaire, I created four groups of fathers, with six additional subgroups; just from the women whose memories of their father were considered mixed or negative.

The four negative father types are: Alcoholics, Abandoners, Abusers and the Emotionally Unavailables. As I read, I found that it was quite common for these women to become involved with men who were either very opposite to their father's personalities or strikingly similar. In fact, their first choice was often their worst. But, mistakes are spiritual opportunities to learn about ourselves and while many women did learn, others are still struggling.

Ignoring, dismissing or denying the impact of your father's influence is a sure sign that you will continue to repeat the pattern of that incomplete or damaged relationship. Look back at your choice of men, delve into their characteristics and consider the type of relationship you created with each one. Ask yourself the following questions.

1. What traits of his did you find most appealing?
2. How did he make you feel?
3. Was he similar or opposite to your father?
4. What did you learn about yourself when the relationship ended?
5. Have you ever become involved with the same type of man more than once?

The men we choose to have relationships with are not chance happenings. Our deep-rooted, unmet needs, compounded by our blatant insecurities, play a powerful role in our selection process. Which brings us right back to our fathers. Understanding your father's childhood, his personality and his frame of mind during many of those troubled years can significantly alter your perception of him. With greater awareness, comes a deeper compassion. And if you're willing, you can take this to a place of understanding, and ultimately to resolution. This is a process, as it is with many of life's powerful lessons. The best part is, you do not need your father's participation. This course of action requires only your effort.

Through these stories, I have come to appreciate how truly significant our fathers have been to our lives, our choices and most remarkably to our self-esteem. At first glance, it might appear as though I am excluding Mothers, but I am not. Many women know the depth of their mother's impact. But, mothers are not fathers and when it comes to choosing the company of the opposite sex, we tend to think of the same sex parent; whether we are attracting or avoiding. However, there is work being done in the human relations field that suggests we choose a mate depending on which parent was our role model. If your father was your role model, then you might seek out a mate who is more similar to your mother. However, this study did not look at the characteristics of mothers and the relationships we have had with them and judging from the stories received it is clear that fathers have a profound impact on how their daughter's choose their relationships.

I hope you find these stories as interesting and revealing as I did. Maybe, you'll find one that reminds you of your own.

SHARI R. JONAS

When
Daddies Drink

9

> *God grant me the serenity to accept the things I cannot change*
> *The courage to change the things I can*
> *And the Wisdom to know the difference*
>
> — The AA Creed

O f all the groups in this study, adult children of alcoholics have had the lion's share of research and public awareness. Thanks to the pioneering efforts of Margaret Cook and the ground-breaking work of Dr. Janet G. Woititz.

In all fairness to the fathers in this chapter, alcoholism is considered a disease. However, its cure cannot be found in a syringe or scribbled on a prescription pad. It is a life-long battle, which begins by surrendering yourself to a higher spirit.

For the children of alcoholics, their suffering can also be life long. Many women make the mistake of choosing boyfriends and husbands who are themselves alcoholics, repeating the vicious cycle of their childhood. One would suspect that these women would know better, having lived with the illness in their home for their entire childhood. Repeating family habits is a common and often times, purposeful custom amongst all families. What then, is the rationale for sustaining and replicating negative family patterns? Some do because they know no other way of life, while others are reliving an experience hoping to make it right.

As you read these stories, you will notice that while some girls break the cycle, many more struggle with it every day. The need to break unhealthy family cycles is a challenge that many of us face throughout our lives. Surprisingly we have a lot more in common with the girls in this group than most of us would have thought. Take a good look at the thirteen characteristics that Dr. Woititz researched and documented. You might notice behavioral patterns which remind you of yourself. Use a pencil and as you read, check off how many of these qualities apply to you (whether or not your father was an alcoholic).

13 Characteristics of Adult Children of Alcoholics

- I guess at what normal behavior is. ☐
- I have difficulty following a project through from beginning to end. ☐
- I lie when it would be just as easy to tell the truth.. ☐
- I judge myself without mercy. ☐
- I have difficulty having fun. ☐
- I take myself very seriously. ☐
- I have difficulty with intimate relationships. ☐
- I over react to changes over which I have no control. ☐
- I constantly seek approval and affirmation. ☐
- I usually feel different from other people. ☐
- I am super-responsible or super-irresponsible. ☐
- I am extremely loyal, even in the face of evidence that the loyalty is undeserved. ☐
- I am impulsive. I tend to lock myself into a course of action ☐
  without giving serious consideration to alternative behaviors
  or possible consequences. This impulsively leads to confusion,
  self-loathing and loss of control over my environment.
  In addition, I spend an excessive amount of energy cleaning
  up the mess.

In 1977, a small group of Alcoholics Anonymous members from New York City discovered that they were all *children of alcoholics* and formed their own Children of Alcoholics meeting. Rather than turning to someone else's research to define their common personality types, they developed their own list. Here are a few of their characteristics that they suggest might result from being brought up by an alcoholic parent.

Again, using your pencil, check off which qualities apply to you.

- I have become an approval seeker (people pleaser) ❏
  and have lost my identity in the process.

- I've either become an alcoholic, married an alcoholic ❏
  or both. Or, I found another compulsive personality,
  such as a workaholic to fulfil my sick abandonment needs.

- I live life from the viewpoint of a victim and I'm attracted ❏
  to that weakness in others.

- It is easier for me to be concerned with others rather ❏
  than myself (hence, my overdeveloped sense of responsibility).
  This enables me not to look too closely at my faults, etc.

- I get guilt feelings when I stand up for myself instead of ❏
  giving in to others.

- I confuse love and pity and tend to love people I can ❏
  pity and rescue.

- I've become addicted to excitement in all my affairs, ❏
  preferring constant upset to workable relationships.

- I have stuffed [hidden away] my feelings from my traumatic ❏
  childhood and have lost the ability to feel or express my
  feelings because it hurts so much.

- I judge myself harshly and have a very low sense of ❏
  self-esteem.

- I have a dependent personality, terrified of abandonment ❏
  and will do anything to hold on to a relationship in order not to
  experience painful abandonment feelings, which I received from
  living with people who were never there for me emotionally.

- I continue to choose insecure relationship because they ❏
  match my childhood relationship with my alcoholic parent.

Out of the twenty-four characteristics, how many were you able to check off? If your father was or is an alcoholic, I imagine you've identified with many qualities. However, if your father was not an alcoholic and you still selected quite a few, there is a good reason. What is happening is that having an alcoholic father is very much like having an absent or abusive father. At the end of the day, if your father wasn't an unconditional loving and approving man, with a consistent presence in your life, there were consequences. Your personality, your self-perceptions and many of your choices were affected by your father. I don't believe anyone with first-hand experience would question that. I do believe that many of us would love to know how others have dealt with it. The following stories will help us to understand just what our opportunities can be.

Carrie, 29 years old

My father was the typical alcoholic, workaholic who was never emotionally or physically available. The best words to describe my relationship with my father would be — hot and cold.

One of my most negative memories of my father was when I was in middle school. I would sit with him in the formal living room and wait while he read his paper and drank his coffee. I kept hoping he would talk to me. The silence was quite deafening. I've always disliked my father's stern tone and stare, whenever he would interact with me.

My father has changed. He has been dry for about fifteen years and has become softer. As an adult, I've tried to connect with him, but he's become even more emotionally unavailable.

My first husband was an alcoholic. Anyone after him was also an alcoholic or an addict. But, they were also smart like my father.

My most difficult relationship was with my last boyfriend. He was a functioning alcoholic, sex-addict, you name it. He had a very addictive personality, which drew me in even more. The more messed up they were, the better they looked to me.

My present husband is so different from my dad. He is loving, open, caring and very humble. He does remind me of my dad in some ways. Good ways. He is very intelligent, a hard worker and very honest. My husband is the best thing that has ever happened to me. Or should I say, the best choice I have ever made.

As a result of my relationship with my father, there has always been a void within me. I think I craved my father's love emotionally and physically. Incidentally, I was raped when I was 16 and I do believe that I was trying to get a man's attention.

When I think about my father, believe it or not, I feel great compassion and love. It's almost like I am five years old and still think the world of him.

"Daddy, do you know how much I love you? I want you to know that I forgive you for anything in the past. I want a relationship with you. I need you. Can we work on this? I am willing to do whatever is possible to make this work."

Leslie, 27 years old

My father is ignorant, eccentric, embarrassing, irrational, anxious, nervous and a perfectionist. He's also an alcoholic. He's never been there for me emotionally and has psychological problems stemming from his childhood. He's a southern man with old racist beliefs. He's addicted to money. He's paranoid and feels that even if he has millions, its still not enough and that he's poor. He never buys clothes and wears stuff that's over ten years old with holes in it. He only showers once a week. He smokes, and treats my mother rudely.

I remember him getting drunk, causing scenes and passing out in his dinner plate at restaurants. I remember him peeing in the closet because he thought it was the bathroom. I also remember him putting a gun to his head and saying he should kill himself and my mom saying, "Do it!"

I'm different from my father; I'm not an alcoholic, I am more loving, I am open minded, sensitive, friendly and intuitive. I want my life to be filled with experiences that will shape me as a whole.

My most difficult relationship was with someone who I took on in order to fix. It was this relationship that made me stronger. I realized that I can't change a person and that I would have to like the way they are from the start. When I became a confident person and loved who I was and knew that I would be happy even if I never fell in love — is when I met my husband.

My husband is very different from my father. He is a family man, more loving and affectionate and believes in equality. We are best friends. He likes me for me. He is unlike most men in the world. My husband was a virgin before me and we waited till our wedding night.

I love my dad because he's my dad. He did work hard for us in his life, but I have no respect for him. I just feel sorry for him, for he really doesn't know his children and doesn't treat his wife the way he should.

"Daddy, I hope you find a way to heal yourself from what ails and tortures you so that you can become more spiritual before you die. Quit blaming yourself, get over it and become better!"

Susan, 25 years old

My father was an alcoholic. By the time I was eight years old my mother had enough of his drinking and my parents divorced. Now, they seem to get along with one another. Although my father was physically present, he was mentally absent. My most negative memories of my father were when he was drinking.

I'm different from my father in that I want to be in my children's life, unlike he seems to. I married a man very similar to my father. He drinks a lot. It's a difficult marriage because of his abusiveness and drinking, but I'm staying married for my children.

When I think of my father, I feel happy. It doesn't matter if he's there for me or not, I'm not still his little girl and I love him a lot.

Janie, 28 years old

My father is a recovering alcoholic. I have so many negative memories of him. Most of them had to do with his drinking. As a young child, our relationship was basically non-existent. He yelled a lot and was very separated [emotionally distant] from the rest of the family. Basically, he was just mean, angry and unloving.

He has changed, though. He's stopped drinking and does try to talk to us. In his own way, he has tried to have a relationship me, as an adult. My most positive memory of him was that he came to the hospital for the birth of my second child.

I am different from my father in that I let my children know how much I love them.

I dated a man who reminded me of my father. There was drug abuse and domestic violence. We never married, but did have a child together. I straightened up and left him when my children's lives were in jeopardy.

As a result of my relationship with my father, I was promiscuous and didn't care how any man treated me. I have had both of my sons out of wedlock with two different men. Both were failed relationships. Both were abusive, one was a drug addict.

The man who is most opposite to my father became my husband. He is caring and understanding, loving and affectionate. I married him because of how we compliment each other's personalities and our lives. I finally realized that I am worth respecting.

When I think about my father, I feel hurt, resentment, anger and frustration. And yet, I forgive him, I love him and I don't blame him anymore for my life's mistakes.

Nicole, 25 years old

My father was a violent and demanding drunk. He was both physically and verbally abusive toward my mother. He was often manipulative and threatening. The only time he was around me was when he wanted me to convince my mom to let him back into the house. He tried to get better but the alcohol would always get the best of him.

My father was like a Dr. Jekyl and Mr. Hyde. When he was sober, he was very intelligent, charming and had quite a presence. Other times, he was cold, austere and unapproachable. When he was drunk, he was very affectionate with me. My most positive memory of my father was when I turned seven he bought me a puppy. What I love most about him was his intelligence and his personality around other people.

My father always demanded that I focused one hundred percent of my attention on school. To seek his approval, I tackled Shakespeare and other literature at a very young age.

My most negative memory of my father was one night when he had been drinking. My mom and I had locked our selves in my room. We had barricaded the door with a large chair and my dad was on the outside trying to come in. He was pushing the door inward and we were holding the chair in place. I remember thinking that we had to keep him out or he would surely kill us.

I'm different from my father in that I don't drink, I am not violent, I hate confrontations and I am always there for my daughter and husband.

One of my boyfriends had many similar qualities to my father. The drinking, the intelligence, the same birthday, same height just to name a few. It was my most difficult relationship because he was very demanding, inconsiderate, manipulative and not giving at all. It ended when I became pregnant. He ran away.

Because my father was abusive, I always thought that it was a result of something I had done. I looked for men that were similar in personality traits as well as physical traits. I was with men who drank and could not control their temper — just like my Dad. I would get an adrenaline rush because of it. I always gave more because I thought I deserved very little. Once I became pregnant and other person's life was involved, I realized that I was in danger of ending up with a man exactly like my father.

At that point, I consciously made an effort to look for someone that had nothing in common with my father — good or bad.

My husband is very opposite to my father. He is hard-working, doesn't drink, doesn't smoke and would never raise a hand to me. He listens to what I say and is supportive in every aspect of my life.

When I think about my father, I feel anger, guilt, frustration, concern, rage and ask a thousand questions. "Daddy, you have hurt me a lot and as a result I have a lot of issues to deal with. I never understood why you could not choose us over the alcohol. Despite it all, I love you. I just wish that you would let me. Your intelligence and knowledge has always inspired me to learn more and more. Although you were affectionate only when you were drunk, I'm glad you were anyway, because now I am comfortable showing people my feelings. Although I am mad at you still, I hope that one day, you find peace within yourself."

Sarah, 32 years old

My father was an alcoholic for thirty something years. As a child, I remember my father being drunk on the weekends and sober during the week. My most negative memory of my father is of him drinking, cursing and being mean. Although my parents are still married, their relationship is terrible. My mother has a lot of resentment towards my father. They are both miserable with one another and have been for a very long time.

When I was eighteen years old, I finally began to know my father. He became sober. He's involved and interested in me now, where before he couldn't think past the beer. This is what I love most about my father now.

Growing up, I was dead set about being with anyone who drank. However, I ended up marrying an alcoholic. Only after we married, I discovered that he was an alcoholic. He's also like my father in that he has low self-esteem. Eventually, I got tired of his drinking and abuse. I needed to change just so that I wouldn't end up in a marriage like my parents.

When I think about my father, I have mixed emotions. I love him now, but still wonder why he put alcohol before his family. It completely blows my mind. "Daddy, I love you and I am so happy that you changed before it was too late for us."

Nancy, 36 years old

My father was an alcoholic and a disciplinarian. As a very young child, I remember being afraid of him. Now we get along great. He is more like a friend to me than a father. He knows that he cannot tell me what to do, so he doesn't even try. If someone is calm and relaxed, I don't believe they love me. I need to be shouted at, then I feel like they care. My ex-husband was an alcoholic who was mentally abusive towards me. I seem to attract alcoholics (like my father) because I feel the need to save people; like a project to work on.

Tanya, 22 years old

My father is an alcoholic. He's never been around for my mother and myself. We fought constantly and over the smallest things. I have been careful with the guys I've gotten involved with. I refuse to have anything to do with men who drink.

"You have treated me like crap my entire life. I deserve better and so does Mommy. I've tried to help you stop. I've even suggested support groups. But your drinking and your friends were always more important. I have no respect for you and very little love, if any. If I never saw you again, it wouldn't be too soon."

Marian, 40 years old

My father was a recovering alcoholic, who died at the age of forty-two, of a massive heart attack after five years of sobriety. I have never had a relationship with a man in which alcohol wasn't a factor. I tend to pick good guys with bad problems. Then, I try to save them and look for approval in inappropriate ways.

"Daddy, I wish that we would have had more time to develop a better relationship. I know in my mind that you always loved me. I just wish that I would have had a chance to feel it and appreciate it. I am older now and I realize how hard your life was. I am also a parent and I understand now how much you sacrificed your life for your children. Thank you."

When
Daddies Walk

10

Let us not look back in anger or forward in fear,
but around in awareness.

' — James Thurber

Have you ever seen a little child lost in a crowded place? One minute ago, she was walking with her parent and the next minute she is standing all alone. The look of fear on her face is unforgettable. Her mind keeps wondering, where must she go, what must she do, whom can she turn to? We always assume that the child must have wandered away. But, what would we think of the parent if it were he who walked away?

To abandon a child is the longest punishment a parent could ever carry out. That is exactly what a child feels when her daddy removes himself from his daughter's life. It is the ultimate rejection. "My daddy didn't love me enough. Not enough to live with me, not enough to watch me grow up, not enough to even call." Any excuse she's been told as to why he had to leave will never satisfy her. She believes, with all her heart that he left because there wasn't anyone worth staying for. She knows how much she loves her dolls, her toys and even her daddy. And, she can never imagine leaving them behind. So, it must be that her father never loved her, at least not enough to stay.

The little girl grows into a woman, but part of her never does. She longs for her daddy's return and with every relationship, she's hoping he's the one. The one who will make her feel worthy again. She wants

SHARI R. JONAS

to hear that he loves her and will never, ever leave. But, she is so insecure that she either drives him away, or beats him to the punch. Isn't it better to walk away than to be the one left behind? "Not again," she thinks. "No one will ever abandon me again." So, she selects men who are not suited for her. It makes the departure so much easier. But, deep down inside, she's not even sure she can attract a really special guy. Remember, her own daddy didn't think she was good enough — why would anyone else?

A young girl takes her daddy's departure so personally and yet, it has so little to do with her. Leaving the children behind can be the most difficult part. Which is why divorce is not just about a marriage ending, but more to do with a family breaking up. There are many dads who leave the house, but do not desert their children. While others do so quite easily. As damaging as divorce is, how a father handles his relationship with his daughter can either heal some wounds or add insult to injury. But once he remarries, feel neglected, rejected and replaced; worse than ever. Why can't a daddy who has deserted his family ever change his mind and come running home? The hardest part of all is when the reality sets in, when he rarely calls, barely visits, misses memorable events or simply remarries.

Abandoning Fathers

Cara, 26 years old
My parents divorced when I was eight years old. He moved away when I was twelve and I didn't see him again until I was twenty-two years old. He would call or write maybe once a year.

My most negative memory of my father is that every time he promised to call, write, pick me up or send me a birthday present, he didn't. What I dislike most about him is his complete lack of concern with anything other than what he wanted. I'm different from my father in that I have compassion for others and interest in my child's life. I want my daughter to have the type of stability that wasn't provided for me.

I was married by the time I was seventeen. Prior to that, I had only two relationships. Both boys reminded me of my father. My most difficult and most successful relationship is with my husband. His love for me is very apparent, although he's just like Dad in a lot of ways. I often have flashbacks of·Dad and how he and Mom interacted. It's very similar to my marriage. My husband can be very manipulative and very selfish when he wants to be.

As a result of my relationship with my father, I seem to find men that have all or most of the qualities that I disliked in my father. When I think about him, I feel anger, rage, hurt, sadness, pity and suspicion. "I'm tired of being hurt by you over and over. Your rejection of me has made me doubt my self-worth and now your rejection of my daughter has made those feelings stronger. I'll never understand why you left me, why you didn't come to my wedding, why you made no effort to meet your own granddaughter until she was four years old. How could you have left me without even checking periodically to see if I was all right? When you finally did contact me and I told you how things were with the newest stepfather, why didn't you help me? Why didn't you ever pay child support? Was I so unimportant to you that you didn't care if I had good clothes to wear or food to eat? Were your own needs and addictions more important to you? How dare you saddle me with these feelings and then refuse the responsibility. Why do you insist on acting as if these last fifteen years never happened and expect me to act the same? Don't offer me anymore lame excuses for your shortcomings, just be a man and admit you were wrong."

Elizabeth, 27 years old

The relationship between my father and me has never been good. When he and my mother separated, we were almost completely out of his life. We would only see him when we were bad and my mother could not control us. She would take us to see him and he would sit us down. Even though he never hit us, the look in his eyes and the firmness of his voice would scare the hell out of us. I remember seeing my mother cry with her friend, telling her all the degrading things he used to do and say to her.

I have only seen my father a few times. Actually, I lived with him for a couple of months. He couldn't handle me so he called my mother to come and pick me up. About eight months ago, I saw him, after not speaking to him for seven years. I called him. He cried the first time he heard my voice on the phone. But, when I went to see him, I felt the same way he always made me feel. I am simply not part of his life. So, I haven't called him since then and never will.

What I dislike most about my father was that he made us kiss his hand every time we would go to see him. It was no longer a hug or even a kiss on the cheek. We had to kiss him on the hand, like he was the king.

I'm different from my dad in that I show and teach my kids respect and not fear. Family comes first. Love is caring, not hurting.

My husband is completely opposite to my father. He is very humble, loving and caring. He believes in family values. He believes in growing old with our children, in watching them grow. To my husband, family comes first.

When I think about my father, I feel anger, resentment, sadness, rage and pain. "Daddy, how could you have left us? You changed my life. I used to cry when I was little, when I used to see my friends holding hands with their dads or hear them talking about how great their father was. You did not give us a chance to have a normal family, to love you and to teach you how to love us. I am so glad that your wife left you and your two adorable kids, just like you left my mother and us. I enjoyed seeing the way you suffered. Most of all, I enjoy knowing that you're going to grow old alone. That is what you deserve. I hope I will never see you again."

Olivia, 32 years old

I have never seen my parents in the same room. My mother got pregnant and he bailed. I used to imagine what it would be like to meet him. Father's day, daddy/daughter dinners, etc., they were awful. I always felt like an outcast. I finally hooked up with my him through a chance encounter with his brother. When this happened, we established a tenuous relationship, at best. I can't think of a specific time where I can recall a positive memory. It's just that I finally had a dad — someone to send a necktie to on father's day. And I did. My most negative memory of my father has to do when I asked him for money. It was only $300 for two weeks, to help me pay my rent. I had sold my old car, but the bank was holding the check for ten days. He said, "No, because you won't pay me back and then there will be hard feelings." Too late, I thought. It was the beginning of the end. I should mention that he has three step-children whom he raised and paid much more on rehab, bail and tattoo removal than what I was asking him for. If it sounds bitter, it's because it is. It's also true. What I dislike most about him is that he is selfish, greedy, judgmental and arrogant. He is quite successful and believes that's what makes or breaks a person — their finances. Of course, I never asked him for money again. After that one time, I learned my value to him.

I'm different from my father. I base my opinions on a person's attributes — whether they are kind, bright, loving, loyal and honest. These things are important to me. They have no value to my father. Aside from money, being in physical shape really matters to him. I am overweight and he sees that as a sign of failure to discipline myself. He has never said it out loud, but it shows in his attitude.

Presently, I am in therapy. Most of my early relationships were spent looking for the love my father never gave me. The later ones, I spent trying to prove that successful men could love me, too.

I dated a man for three years whom I later realized, was very similar to my father. He was successful, intelligent and

SHARI R. JONAS

emotionally crippled, unable to give of himself. Like many of them, he abandoned me.

My second husband was completely opposite to my father. He was so loving. Although he was very immature and an all-around loser, he wrote me love poems and held me every day. He really did love me. It was nice for a while, but it wasn't enough.

One of my boyfriends taught me what real love and respect is. Now, I will never be with a man who doesn't treat me with love and dignity. I loved this man like I have never loved anyone in my life. He said he loved me too, but couldn't cope with intimacy. I think that is what attracted me to him. His aloofness. Though he was patient and listened to me, he could not give back. He ended the relationship three years ago.

As a result of my relationship with my father who abandoned me physically, emotionally and financially, so has every man I have ever been with. I always went for the guy who I had to win over; those who were stand-offish and cool. I would chase them until I felt that I had made them love me.

When I think about my father, I feel pain, followed by anger and then a sense of loss — of what could have been. I have finally realized that I was giving too much to my father and getting too little in return. So, I cut off all ties to him. It's been nearly a year. It was just not worth the pain.

Dona, 14 years old

The first time I saw my father was when I was in third grade. It was also the last time. My father is an alcoholic. He lived with us for about a year and then left. Before I knew who he was, I thought he was godly. Now, I think he is a bad person.

As a result of my relationship with my father, I don't get close to people, for fear that they will leave me. I hate feeling vulnerable. When I think about my father, I feel sadness, depression and anger. If I could say anything to him, I'd tell him how much he hurt me.

Ellen, 17 years old.

I haven't had any contact with my father since I was nine years old. Prior to that, he never seemed very interested in my life. Sometimes he would take me out and sometimes he just never showed up when he said he would. There is really nothing I love about my father. What I dislike most about him is that he has never tried to get in touch with me over the last few years, especially now that I am about to go to college.

I'm different from my father. I finish what I start. He left me because he had me at such a young age. But I didn't desert my daughter when I had her. Even my boyfriend didn't leave me when he found out I was pregnant. He was eighteen years old at the time. It's been two years and we're still together. He shows me that he loves me and cares for me.

As a result of my father's absence, I craved male attention. I flaunted myself so that I could get it. Then, I ended up sleeping around from thirteen to fifteen years of age. I just wanted to be loved by a man.

When I think about my father, I feel anger, sadness, fear that I will never see him again, sorrow for what he has missed and pity that my daughter will never know him.

"I wish that you would have been here for me all these years. It would have been nice if you had encouraged me when I was pregnant. I wish you could be here to see me graduate high school. The only thing you've ever done is give me half of your genes."

Ashley, 18 years old

I really didn't know my father. My parents divorced when I was two years old. I remember having to go and visit him. I felt like I had to see him, that I had no choice. I also felt that he really didn't want to see me. As I got older, I saw him when I wanted to — which was only about three times. We didn't have a relationship.

Recently, my father has started to change. Now, he wants a relationship with me. We've discussed the past. We both realize

SHARI R. JONAS

that we need to get to know each other first, before we can have a father/daughter relationship.

As a result of my relationship with my father, I see a definite pattern. I didn't trust him and therefore I don't trust any man. I feel as if since my own dad couldn't love me, how could any man.

Thinking about my father, gets me upset and angry because I wish it wasn't this way. "I hate you for leaving and never trying to be my daddy. It didn't have to be this way. We lost a lot of years that didn't have to be lost. I love you and always will, because, you still are my dad."

Linda, 36 years old
The best word to describe my father would be "absent." He worked all the time. When he was around, he was very stern, but affectionate. My father has no back-bone. He lets everyone else take control. He also skirts around issues. I'm different from my father. I take control of the situation and I'm honest and direct.

My parents divorced when I was eleven years old. It was my mother who told my father to leave stating that it was just a matter of time before he would leave. Soon after, he married my mom's best friend.

My father lets his second wife run the house, finances and family decisions. They moved four miles away, however, he never visited us or tried to call.

Although I was my father's little girl, I was not the apple of his eye. I believe he tried to win my older sister's affections.

I've never dated a man like my father and I've never had a successful relationship. All the men I have dated were either convicted felons or unemployed. Whereas my father has never committed a crime in his life and has always worked very hard.

My most difficult relationship ended when he told me he honestly didn't love me and was leaving the state with another woman. Every once in a while he would come around. The only way I could get rid of him permanently was to sleep with his brother. So I did, for two years. He never came back.

As a result of my relationship with my father, I seem to date men who have other priorities. I always come in third or fourth place because of their lifestyles.

When I think of my father, I feel emptiness, anger, sadness, disappointment and abandonment.

When Daddies Remarry

Sue, 34 years old
Between five and fifteen years of age, I lived with my father. When his new wife came along, I was sent away from my father's home to live with my mother. I was twelve years old. Since then, there's been little communication, no matter how hard I've tried. I've also been alienated from his present family. I am angry with my father. When I was younger, I wanted to be with men who were basically unavailable to me or men that would eventually hurt me or abandon me. I often found myself pushing men away before they got too close. I never wanted to be physically abused, but I was young and naïve. I also believed that we could work it out. I was wrong. My first husband was like my father in many ways; physically and mentally abusive, incapable of showing love, same age and both interested in cars. My current husband is loving and attentive. We do almost everything together and he is genuinely concerned with every aspect of my life. He's assumed the role of father to my son and loves him the same as his own. My husband is not afraid to show his love for me. No matter where we are or what we're doing, he always lets me know that he's there for me and I trust that he'll always be. My father never abused me physically or mentally. Is emotional neglect considered abuse? Although I've never had a relationship with my father, I feel as if I'm missing something because my father's not in my life. But, I don't know what.

Melanie, 21 years old

My parents divorced when I was two years old. My dad was not in the picture very much after he married his second wife. As a young girl, I really don't remember seeing him very often. I used to become very upset when he wouldn't show up to watch me play softball and soccer. When I was eleven years old, I asked to move in with him. He said that I could. My older brother had lived with him for a little while and I wanted the same opportunity. While I lived there, it was as if I was living alone, even though we were in the same house. We never spoke. I would even go without eating because his wife would fix dinner for her and dad and not make me anything. I didn't feel very wanted by his wife. By the time I was thirteen years old, she had a baby. After that, I was really out of the picture. I saw my dad with the new baby and I was very jealous because he never spent that kind of time with me. I did love that child like it was my own. Two years later, the baby died.

I always wanted to do things with my dad, but he was either at work or drinking. It seemed like drinking was his number one priority. The only real positive memory I have with my father was when he took me out in a big truck that he had. We went digging through the back woods. I'm like my Dad in that we both have a hard time telling the people that we love, that we love them.

My dad treated my older brother differently. He would do more guy things with him As my brother got older, they seemed to have more to say to one another. I got into sports hoping that we would have something to talk about. I liked all the teams that my Dad liked. I even played very rough with him and would be strong, even when he hurt me. I tried to like everything that he liked.

I love my Dad because he is my Dad. I love everything about him. But, there are ways about him that I wish were different. He didn't show me any love at all. I tried so hard for him to love me. No matter what I did, it seemed as if I could never get his attention.

He has changed a bit. But only because I have reached the age of twenty-one and I go to the local bar where he drinks. I see him a little more than I used to, but when I do he is usually drunk. He becomes a different person when he is drinking, more physical. He'll grab me and hug me — but in a playful way.

In the past, I dated men who were older than me and some of them would drink like my dad. The most difficult relationship I ever had was one of my first serious ones. I was fifteen years old and he was twenty-eight. He drank, smoked and did drugs. He hit me twice. He treated me badly and cheated on me. He got me pregnant and left me. I had an abortion and then he wanted me back. I was so hurt and felt so bad for what I had done. I knew that I would have to live with this decision for the rest of my life. I wanted him to feel the pain that I had felt. So, I went back to him for a short period of time and then left him. I wanted to be the one to finally end it.

The man I am with now does not drink or smoke. He loves his children and tells them so every chance he gets. He also wants the people around him to be happy. He has tried to show me how much he loves me and treats me very well. He tries to understand why I am the way that I am. He is very loving and is ready to start a new life together. I feel as if he is the right one for me. We've been together for three years.

When I think about my father I get sad. How I wish things were different back then and different now. I am jealous of my father's wife. She doesn't love him like I do, yet she gets to see him more. She treats him badly. The only reason they are still together is because he doesn't want to put my little brother through what I went through. It might also have to do with money.

"Daddy, why didn't you show me any love when I was growing up? Why can't you show me love now? You never told me that you loved me more than five times in my life. Why not? You say that you do not want my little brother raised the way my older brother and I were. Why are you so worried about him and weren't worried about us? All I ever wanted was for you to tell me that you loved me and that you were glad that I was a part of you. Why couldn't you show me that? Why couldn't you tell me?"

SHARI R. JONAS

Vicky, 40 years old

For years, my father never showed up when he was supposed to and I always remember being disappointed. Strangely enough, when I was eight years old, he insisted that my sister and I live with him. He promised me everything under the sun. However, when my grades began dropping and I started getting into trouble (problems that every teenager goes through) he sent me back to my mother. He said that my step-mother couldn't handle it. Then, he just drifted in and out of our lives. About four years ago, he got married for the third time. Although I wasn't invited to the wedding, I showed up anyway, only to be publicly humiliated and excluded from his new family. Even my half sister, from his previous marriage was included in the ceremony. But, my sister and I were not. Quite a slap in the face, huh?

My first husband reminded me of my father. He ran at every opportunity he got when it came time to being responsible for our children. My present fiancé is completely opposite to my father. He is a wonderful man who cares about how I feel. Although my children are not his, he treats them as his own. He spends time with my children. We're a family, for the first time.

My relationship issues always revolve around trust. I have never been able to open up to anyone. I'm sure this has caused problems for me.

"Daddy, why did you turn your back on me? Why have you always pushed me out the door when you bring a new family into your life? Not just once, but over and over! Why did you always treat me like you never loved me? I will never allow my children to feel the way you have made me feel!"

Marnie, 42 years old

My parents divorced when I was less than one year old. My father remarried and my step mother actively worked to get me him away from me. Our relationship was odd, sort of separated by glass. I saw him occasionally, but I couldn't reach him. When I was thirty six years old, my step mother died. My father came to my porch to visit my new baby daughter and me. That was our first real moment together. Since then, we have both built on that moment. Today we continue to have a rich, emotional life. I think he takes as much pleasure in it as I do. It's interesting how grateful I am. I waited an entire lifetime for this. It's really never too late.

"Daddy, I missed you so very much as a young child. I think you are the most wonderful father in the world. I just wish I could have had your hugs as a little girl. But, I am grateful for how much I have with you today. Sadly, it will never take away from what I yearned for as a child".

Tara, 33 years old

When I was young, I remember my father always being very sad. Up until the age of four, I believed I was Daddy's little girl. Then my parents divorced. It seemed as though my father projected some of his feelings about my mom onto me. My father remarried when I was around 10 and then our relationship really changed. He was intent on keeping his new marriage and had no intention of me causing any conflict. So, with a lot of anger and resentment, we slowly parted. We were working on some issues right up until he became ill. My father passed away three years ago.

My most negative memory of my father was of him telling me how awful my mom was and that I would end up just like her. My father always seemed to play the role of 'poor me' to the hilt. He never took responsibility for what he created emotionally. I'm different from my father in that I am very open with my feelings. I, on the other hand, believe in taking complete responsibility for what I create. Furthermore, I do not allow a partner to become the center of my life.

As a result of my relationship with my father, I found myself needing approval from men and testing those who loved me. "Daddy, I'm sorry. Sorry that you were so sad and sorry if I ever made you sad. I want you to know that you hurt me because you never loved me and you didn't believe in me. Even though I hope that you are happy and at peace now, I do resent the fact *that you left me with such a mess to clean up. I realize that you must have thought that I was strong enough to deal with things. But, it would have been nice to have you tell me this in some other way. I am still very angry and hurt, more than you will ever know."*

Becky, 24 years old

My dad was my hero. I loved him more than anyone in the world. He made me feel protected and secure. When he was happy, I was happy. I would have done anything to please him. I always wanted to be daddy's little girl, but he loved my sister just a little bit more than me. Probably because she didn't chase after his attention like I did. He always had to beg her to talk to him, but I would sit at his feet and wait for him to talk to me.

My Dad remarried about ten years ago and within three years that woman had destroyed every relationship my father had with his children. He doesn't speak to anyone of us. He has six grandchildren and no contact with any one. The last time I spoke to my father was when my grandmother died three years ago. My sister and I were not allowed to sit with my father because his wife doesn't like us. We were treated like outcasts.

I have so much difficulty trusting guys. My dad let me down and it's too hard for me to feel secure with anyone.

"Dad, why did you choose "her" over your children and grandchildren? Why didn't you at least come to us and try to work things out? How could you just cut us out of your life? Were we that easy to dispose of? Do you miss us at all? I hate the way I feel inside because of you. I don't even have a father to give me away at my wedding. Doesn't that matter to you? Give me some answers. Please don't let me enter into my marriage carrying all this around with me."

11

When
Daddies Detach

The greatest part of our happiness or our misery depends
not upon our circumstances, but upon our disposition.
— Martha Washington

F ood and water are our most essential nutrients; the absence of
either would surely have a detrimental effect on our physiological
well-being. However, there is compelling evidence indicating we
have additional vital and fundamental needs.

For the past thirty-five years, researchers have studied attachment
in infants and the importance of attachment for later years. The results
of their work indicate that infants, given the choice between attention
and stimulation or food and water, show more attachment behavior to
the adult who is providing the attention and stimulation. The importance of attachment in infants was supported by additional studies,
which found that toddlers with secure and emotional attachments
demonstrated more trust and confidence later in life. True stories of
children locked up in rooms and cages for years on end are further
evidence an infant needs more than just food and water to develop into
a happy and well-adjusted member of society.

Unconditional love, emotional availability, physical affection,
security, consistency and trust are the prerequisites for a healthy,
emotional life. With the fulfilment of these basic human needs, an
individual can develop a wonderful sense of self-worth, self-esteem and
compassion. Without these essential elements, a human being will not

SHARI R. JONAS

die, but the quality of their emotional and social development will be affected until that individual learns to self-administer these qualities.

Allow me to explain. A child who is feeling unloved or unwanted does not have the capacity to boost their spirits and inject purpose-fullness into their existence. They rely on their parent or caregiver for the assurance that they are loved and cared for. Without the input and effort of a significant adult, the child's emotional state becomes burdened with sadness, loneliness, feelings of inadequacy and insecurity.

As this child matures into a young adult, her need for love, affection, attention and approval defines her character and undermines every relationship she engages in. It's only a matter of time before she begins to learn how to use her body in the futile attempt to fulfil her unmet needs. When relationships last longer than a one-night stand, she tends to fall in love easily, tolerates unacceptable behavior, changes aspects of herself to please her partner and has difficulty walking away from the relationship, when she knows she should. Her insecurity skyrockets, while her self-esteem plummets. What will it take for her to realize that another human being, especially of the opposite sex, can never fill the void that her daddy left behind?

Having a father who is emotionally unavailable is a double-edged sword; he is both present and absent. She sees her daddy, he exists in her life, but he never says, "I love you." Isn't he supposed to? She can play around with different ideas to defend his cold demeanor. He works a lot, he's more comfortable with the boys in the family, he and Mom fight so much that he always seems to be in a bad mood. But, in the end, that little girl believes that her daddy never showed his love, never took an interest in her life and never made her feel special because he didn't want to. He could have — she was right there all along, waiting for him to shower her with warmth. Yet, he never did. He was there, but he was absent.

Many of the fathers in this study fall under this description. A father can be emotionally unavailable from one's earliest memories or he might have become that way as a result of divorce, second marriage or the onset of his daughter's puberty. The reasons for his behavior are not as important as the consequences.

There is a place within every little girl's heart that is reserved for her daddy's love. If he is unable to demonstrate his love, even remotely, that place becomes a void. The little girl will grow up and rather than feeling the emptiness, will attempt to fill the hole in her heart. She might fall in love with bad boys, sleep with older men, develop an eating disorder or work painstakingly at her job to prove she's worthy. And still, she finds herself incredibly unhappy.

What will it take to break her destructive patterns? Must she hit rock bottom before she realizes how much the absence of her daddy's love has affected her life? Rock bottom might mean depression, a bad reputation, anorexia, obesity, unemployment or divorce. It's different for everyone. Yet, the end result is the same; sheer unhappiness. But, it doesn't have to be that way. She can put an end to her self-deprecating, destructive behaviors by recognizing its roots. What is she searching for? What hole is she desperately and inappropriately trying to fill? Doesn't she realize she's only punishing herself? She must come to understand that to move forward, she must look forward, rather than dwelling in the past, longing for a love she never received. Easy to say, hardest to do. One small step at a time, is the best that anyone can do. Personal progress is determined not just by a willingness to change, but by the slightest act of improving one's self, one's thoughts and one's behavior.

If tomorrow you discovered that your daddy really loved you and was very proud of you, what part of you would change? If you never hear those words are you destined to remain the person that you are today? If so, that's a lot of power that you've handed over to another human being, power that you could turn inward, to give you the strength, courage and wisdom to improve even the smallest aspect of yourself.

The child who suffered without her daddy's love and approval is all grown up now. She can, if she wants to, provide herself with unconditional love. She can accept her imperfections, nurture her basic needs and rebuild her self- esteem. She can . . . if she wants to.

Cynthia, 34 years old

I really have no words to describe my father, other than he was "there". My father had a vague presence in the family. He was emotionally absent. He seemed to keep us at arms' length. He never asked how we were doing in school, with friends or anything related to general everyday life. He was always on the fringes of my life. He really never knew what was happening in my life, wasn't even interested in anything that had to do with me. He really showed no interest in me. He was nice enough, I guess. Only rarely did he really show any love to me. Otherwise, he was like an acquaintance.

My parents did not have a loving marriage. My mother tried very hard, despite the problems between them. But, my father was never affectionate or loving. He cheated on my mom a lot. The pain that caused resulted in horrible arguments, which my sisters and I were witness to. I will never forget those fights. Needless to say, my mother finally could not take it anymore and they agreed upon a divorce.

I have lots of negative memories of my father. What I remember most is how he hurt my mother, said nothing to us and just packed up and left. My father hurt me the few times that he would help me with my homework. He would get frustrated and call me stupid. What I dislike about him most is his inability to acknowledge me as his daughter.

There were times I didn't feel he loved me at all — like when my father would come home from work and not say even one word to me — which is how most days usually went. Most times I felt invisible to him.

I am different from my father in that I have the ability within myself to love someone. I care about my children and their well-being. Unfortunately, I resemble my father in that I can't hold my marriage together, no matter what. I have a problem with fidelity. I feel helpless with this. It keeps happening over and over, no matter what I try to do to prevent it.

My husband is totally opposite to my father. He loves me, he's faithful and he cares very much about me. Although I love my husband of fourteen years, it is a very difficult relationship for me. I can't seem to give my husband all that he needs. Not until I can find it within myself to do so.

I have difficulty letting my husband get too close to me. When I feel he is, it comes across as a controlling feeling, which I tend to rebel against. I have trouble meeting my husband's needs for intimacy. I am unable to be faithful to him. My inability to stay faithful and to be comfortable with him intimately is driving us apart.

As for myself, I am not sure what my husband is unable to provide me — something is obviously lacking due to my tendency to wander outside the marriage. I am usually drawn to men that have a sense of humor. I guess because my husband doesn't and I do. I require laughter, a lot. I enjoy feeling desired by someone. I don't know if maybe it's a power issue. Maybe I just like to have control in a relationship and getting involved with someone new means I can pretty much call the shots.

Recently, my husband and I have separated. I have finally decided to seek counselling. I am determined to find the better side of myself, to find what I have been searching for all these years.

My father was never a dad to me. A dad is a man who shows affection and love. He's someone who asks what's wrong if there's a problem, who helps you if you are having trouble with something, who talks with you about life in general, who cares about you and lets you know it. A dad takes the time to take you places and does things with you. A dad protects you and makes you the center of his life.

When I think about my father I feel a lot of anger. I am angry because I feel I have been cheated on. I feel like I have been given something I did not want or ask for — an emotional problem. All I ever wanted was to be loved and cared for by my father.

I would love to be able to tell my father what I have been wondering all these years. I'd like to ask him why he didn't care for me or about me from the day I was born. Didn't he know that I needed him when I was younger? Doesn't he know that every daughter needs a loving father?

SHARI R. JONAS

Dawn, 30 years old

My parents divorced when I was nine years old. Basically, my father was unavailable and distant. He would talk to me about anything if I called him. But, I very rarely ever heard from him. He was busy with his life and he seemed to go on without my brothers and me. My father has never really been there for me. He spent a lot of time on his hobbies, which were traditionally male-oriented. Naturally, he enjoyed showing his son "the ropes." So, I cut my hair and became a tomboy. I learned about the cars he was interested in and how to put models together. I would watch sports and try to help him whenever he was building something. All of this I did to seek his approval.

My father had a violent temper. Once, my brothers and I staged an injury from a fake fight we had in order to end a fight he and my mother were having. He has changed for the better, though. Mainly for the benefit of his current wife and children. He doesn't have the violent temper anymore and spends a lot of time with my half brother and sister.

I'm different from my father. I spend more time with my child. I am a more positive person than he is. I am more grounded in reality and I don't incur financial debt like he does.

One of my boyfriends reminded me of my father. He was emotionally unavailable, selfish and had a domineering personality. I wanted too much from him. I expected too much. I always had a need for reassurance and I couldn't trust him. I was always afraid that he would leave me . . . and he did.

Another boyfriend was opposite to my father. He wanted to give me everything and was always there for me. I wasn't used to that. I found him to be boring and overbearing.

As a result of my relationship with my father, I have always sought attention and reassurance of love. This has destroyed every relationship I have had with a man, because I couldn't let things be the way they were. I was always pushing for more; more attention, more time together, more love.

Eventually, I became aware of the patterns in my life. I developed a better ability to let go. My self-esteem improved.

I stopped trying to make my boyfriend pay for — or make up for — my father's mistakes and shortcomings. With my present boyfriend, I feel secure and I trust him.

When I think about my father, just about every imaginable emotion comes up. He knows of my disappointments and hurts. They will never change or go away. He will never be the father I want him to be. But, I still love him and accept him for who he is.

Ruth, 37 years old

My father had multiple sclerosis from the time I was born. Although he was a caring man, he was engrossed in his illness. Gradually, I caught on that my father was sick and slowly withdrew from relying on him as a daughter would to her father. I was painfully and acutely aware that I was missing something wonderful that some of my friends had with their fathers. Needless to say, I was very ashamed to have a sick father. It seems that I always need somebody to love. My life feels flat if I don't have a man to feel excited about. When I'm between relationships, I am reaching out and looking out for a new guy to become attached to. The driving force behind this seems to be this ache in my heart. I refer to it as the "hole in my heart." I find myself longing for a man who is attractive yet unavailable. In fact, I spent much of my youth pining over some unavailable guy, much to my distraction and discontentment.

Kimberely, 40 years old

When I was six to seven and nine to ten years old, my father was gone for a year — long tour of duty in Vietnam. Each time that he'd returned, there was a long adjustment period as he tried to take back his power of the household that my mother had assumed while he was gone. I think it was extremely difficult for him to go to Vietnam and then try to come home and be happy. He seemed lost and yet tried to keep control.

During these years, our relationship was very confusing. When he was gone, he'd send us cassette tapes instead of letters and would tell us briefly what was happening in his life. I

SHARI R. JONAS

missed him during that time, but we'd get used to our mother being the boss in the house. When he wanted to, he could be very attentive. He would come to my sporting events, take me to the stables, take me to work with him on weekends, etc. At other times, he would be very distant and very uncommunicative, to a point where we were almost afraid of approaching him. He was very strict, expected us to make A's in school and we were always afraid of disappointing him.

My most positive memory of my father was being involved in his movie production, which he wrote, directed and produced. My most negative memory was having him miss my high school graduation because he was with one of his mistresses. What I dislike most about him was his unavailability and perfectionism.

As a result of my relationship with my father, I have always chosen men who were emotionally unavailable. In turn, I would change myself to the point of losing myself as I tried, unsuccessfully, to please each man. My ex-husband was similar to my father in that he, too, was emotionally unavailable. But, he was different from my father in that he was very family oriented. However, in order to please him, I moved to another country and had to learn a whole new culture and language. I felt very alone and was very unhappy. I couldn't pretend anymore to be the person he wanted me to be and so I left him.

My last relationship was with someone who reminded me of my father. He was selfish, critical and a perfectionist. I tried very hard to change myself to fit his criteria. As a result of the control he had over me, the relationship turned into an obsession and I had to turn to the police for help. I felt emotionally battered by this man. However, that is what it took for me to recognize my pattern, understand myself and begin my healing process. I have been alone for three years since that relationship. I will never allow myself to be treated like that ever again. Nor will I ever change who I am to please another individual.

When I think about my father, I feel sadness, frustration for time lost, bitterness to some degree, but, most of all, sadness.

"Dad, I hope that one day you will understand that family is all we really have in this world and that loving relationships bring more joy then anything else. I know you will never truly understand the damage you have done to me, my sister and my brother during our childhood years. Thank you for being my father, although I missed you growing up and I still miss you now."

Sandra, 33 years old

My relationship with my father has been non-existent. We didn't have a relationship. He worked and when he was home, I must have avoided him. To seek my father's approval, I tried to be as invisible and inconspicuous as possible. I was a chubby little thing and to him that was inexcusable. What I dislike most about my father is the way I felt dismissed by him. I always felt as if I were in the way when I was around him.

Now that I am older, he has more patience and understanding. I think he sees me as more of a person now, than he did before.

I have found myself attracted to men with some of my father's characteristics; hard working, brash, bigoted, tendency to drink. It frightens me to think I may wind up in the same sort of marriage my mother did. I've never had what I would consider a successful relationship. The longest one was two years and that was a mess. He was controlling and abusive, but I was afraid that I would never find anyone else who would love me and so I stayed. Eventually, I decided that living within the guidelines of his tightly-controlled world was not what I wanted for myself or the children that we might have one day. One night, he finally let loose and became more violent than in the past. That was enough to shake any doubts loose and I got out.

There was one relationship that could have been successful but I ended it out of fear of commitment. He was quite different from my father. He was very fair minded. He was more of a white collar guy, who was very concerned with the appearance of his home, his education and furthering himself in life. My dad, on the other hand, acts as if he doesn't care what anyone else thinks of him and enjoys it when he can shock people. This boyfriend was wonderful, but I was afraid at the time, afraid he would love me.

As a result of how my father made me feel, I think I have trouble understanding how someone can love me. That's how I felt as a little girl. I think I have a fear of commitment. I'm afraid that I'll end up in the same type of relationship my parents had. I also have a fear of a relationship ending in divorce.

When I think about my father, I get choked up because I do respect and admire him now. Even though he is not what I would consider an ideal man, I appreciate his presence in my life. What is most frustrating is that we are both unable to show and tell each other how we feel.

"Daddy, I love you and although you were not a model father, I think I turned out okay. I forgive you for the little hurts you caused me. Please take better care of yourself, because I do fear being without you."

Natalie, 18 years old
My parents divorced when I was two years old. I don't really remember much about their marriage except that my father was verbally abusive towards my mother. Presently, they attempt to be friendly. However, my step mother is rather difficult and makes it almost impossible for them to have any contact.

My dad has always been very distant. He's been there for me financially, but has never been very loving. He felt that if he gave me money and material goods, I was all set. He didn't think I needed love and affection. My most positive memory of my father is of him picking me up every now and then and going for lunch. He did this because my mom told him to.

I'm like my father in that I am very distant and keep my feelings to myself. However, unlike him, I am able to show love.

My father treated the boys in the family very differently. He really favored then. It seemed he preferred their presence rather than mine. I tried to seek my father's approval by being successful in sports and school.

My present boyfriend is completely opposite to my father. He is very sensitive, kind hearted and loving. He's capable of showing his love towards me when we're alone and with other people. I have difficulty accepting the affection he shows towards me.

As a result of my relationship with my father, I pick men who are the complete opposite of my father.

When I think about my father, I feel sadness and anger.

"Daddy, why couldn't you ever love me like you loved the boys?"

Julie, 30 years old

My father was someone I knew was in the house on the weekends, but I was never sure where. He went to work every morning at 7:30 and arrived home at 10:00 at night. That's just the way it was, until I was fourteen. Then I became pregnant and he took a more active role in my life. I can see that I've always chosen men who were emotionally unavailable. The therapy that I received has helped me to heal my childhood and improve my relationship with my father. Since then, I have made better choices in lovers. My father has also recognized and apologized for the ways in which he hurt us and has become a more active part of our lives.

 _____

She's taking her time making up the reasons
To justify all the hurt inside
Guess she knows from the smiles and the look in their eyes
Everyone's got a theory about the bitter one
They're saying "Mamma never loved her much"
And, "Daddy never keeps in touch
That's why she shies away from human affection."

— Savage Garden

　　　　　　　　S H A R I   R.   J O N A S

When Daddies Do Damage

12

*In the depth of winter, I finally learned that within me
there lay an invincible summer.*

— Albert Camus

Abuse comes in all shapes and sizes. It is a monster, a shadow, a snake in the grass. It can be as subtle as a windburn or as blatant as a tornado. We can feel it, we can hear it, we can see it, but we have trouble speaking of it. Because, there isn't anything more humiliating than being emotionally, physically or sexually abused by your own flesh and blood. Father is protector; he is the knight in shining armor. But if he can commit such wrongful acts to his innocent, little girl, then who on earth can this child ever trust?

Abuse, in all its forms, is crippling. The body is bruised, the self-esteem is shattered, the heart is broken and the spirit is crushed. What, then, is the prognosis? What kind of life will a grown woman have when her childhood memories consist of painful secrets and dehumanizing tales? You would be surprised.

The women in this study and throughout the world who have suffered at the hands of their fathers have become some of the most successful, productive and positive people you might ever encounter. Their experiences have taught them that strength comes from within. Their resiliency, despite their adversity, is remarkable. Although the pain of their past is etched in their memory banks forever, their attitude and aptitude is on the top of their daily agenda.

Life teaches us lessons in many different ways. The abused child can take that experience and do so much with it. Her character can evolve with a greater sensitivity and a deeper understanding of the world around her. She can touch lives, restore faith and teach the meaning of inner strength. Nobody knows how to survive and thrive, better than a survivor.

Of course, there are many who are still emotionally maimed and paralyzed from their horrible experience. They simply cannot break away from the feelings of loss, humiliation and fear. Loss of their innocence, loss of trust, loss of self-worth, fear of being hurt and a fear of men. They are prisoners within the prison walls of their own mind. However, the key to unlocking their cell has been with them all along. If only they could reach within themselves to a place they've never visited, they will find the key. That place is their spirit.

Every human being is born with a spirit. A boundless energy that is more powerful than any other. It is the provider of strength, guidance, wisdom and love. Look within yourself and you will find your own spirit. Surrender yourself to yourself. Thousands upon thousands of victims of abuse manage their traumas, achieve inner happiness and exceed their own expectations. You can too, once you realize that you have been walking around with the key to your freedom. It's up to you to decide when you will finally put it to use

When Daddies Bruise

Sheila, 36 years old
My father always beat me and said I was good for nothing. Once, when I was a little girl, he came to the playground and starting kicking me like I was a garbage can. All my friends were there. My ex-husband would beat me and my girls up and say we were good for nothing, too.

"Daddy, I wish you would stop saying that I am good for nothing."

SHARI R. JONAS

Liz, 34 years old

How would I describe my father? He is a mean, angry, distant, unfeeling, uncaring, dominating, controlling man. He puts others down. Things always had to be done his way or they were done wrong. My dislike for my father is so strong, it borders on hate. He didn't protect me. Rather, he instilled great fear in me from verbal and physical abuse. I used to pray that he'd come home safely, and then I used to pray that he wouldn't come home at all.

My father has a very bad temper and constantly yelled at my sister and me about everything. We never measured up to his standards. I developed such anger and hate towards him, of which I am unable to let go. I find it difficult to believe that he did the best that he could in raising me, because he was never interested in learning how to be a better person or parent. No one was allowed to tell him he needed help or could suggest how to get it. I was not allowed to express my emotions and to this day have a hard time doing so — especially crying.

I don't know that I've ever loved my father. I know that I do not like him as a person. I don't see anything positive about him at all. I can't even recall a kind, loving or fatherly moment with him. I don't know if that is because I am blocking them from memory or if it is because there really weren't any.

My most negative memory of my father is of him hitting me, putting me down and taking off on the family for hours on end. My father just didn't care enough about being a father to learn how to do a better job. He also never admits to his mistakes.

A father is supposed to protect his children. Mine never did this. In particular, as a teenager a friend's father abused me. My father didn't do anything to protect me from this man or from any further contact, preferring to ignore it instead. I need to learn to forgive my father for these things as they are having a negative affect on my life and I don't want them to have that control over me any longer.

The difference between my father and myself is that I have a sincere desire to better myself. I am also loyal, trustworthy, *approachable, kind, understanding and dedicated. Basically, my father's priorities were himself, reading the newspaper, watching television and being left alone.*

I dated a man that was completely opposite to my father for five years. He was sensitive, open, loving, kind. He shared his emotions, he shared his struggles, he asked for help. He was (unlike my father) a protector.

What do I feel when I think of my father? Hate, anger, fear and sadness. As a child and teenager, I disliked him very much. I still do not like my father. But, because he is my father I have kept him in my life. If he were not my father, I would have absolutely no contact with him.

"Why didn't you care enough about me to be a good dad? Why didn't you ever listen to me? Why did you put the kids from church before me? How can you be disappointed in me when you see me acting like you? Yet, you never tried to better yourself and help me better myself. You only put blame on me and never accepted your role in how I turned out."

Penny, 32 years old

I have three words to describe my father: scary, violent and abusive. My father used to beat us. As a child, I hated him. While my parents were married, all I witnessed was violence and hate. He was physically and emotionally abusive. When I was eight years old he held me down and put a diaper on me on my mom's birthday because I burnt her bologna sandwich. When I was ten years old, I caught him having sex in the back seat of a car.

My father loved himself more than anyone. He was selfish and a hypocrite. He physically and sexually abused me. He was and still is a Baptist Minister.

For so many years, I was attracted to people who treated me badly because I never thought that I was worthy of someone treating me good. I was intimidated by anyone who was different from my dad. I knew how to handle an abusive relationship. I didn't know how to handle or keep a healthy one. Abuse was my perception of norm.

SHARI R. JONAS

My ex-husband was one of many men who reminded me of my father. He, too, was a selfish, self-centered human being who was neither intelligent nor cultured. Neither was willing to pay child support and both were spoiled by their mothers. My ex continually betrayed me and at the cost of our daughter. Eventually, I fell into a major depression and with the support of a therapist, I got the courage to leave my marriage.

My present husband is completely opposite to father. He is a father and a role model to my daughter from a previous marriage. He has literally sacrificed his career to be a father to his daughter who had moved out of state. He is stable, hard-working, honest, distinguished and morally forthright.

When I think of my father, I feel anger, guilt, shame disgust, confusion and more guilt. Should I forgive and forget? I tried to have a relationship with him two years ago. Even then, everything in my life he felt the need to compete with, instead of feeling a sense of parental pride for my success. He continually expects me to reach out to him and apologize. Yet, he has never apologized to me.

Elaine, 38 years old

My father was the enforcer, the one who decided the punishment. He wasn't available for anything else. He believed that children should be seen and not heard. He always said no to anything that was fun. He was racist, strict, narrow-minded and self absorbed. The world revolved around him.

My father would beat me with a belt and tell me to stop crying or he'd give me a reason to cry. When I became desensitized to these beatings, I decided that I wouldn't give him the satisfaction of seeing me cry. Then I realized that the longer I put off crying, the more I got beaten. It was an awful situation. If I didn't cry that was a sign to beat me more. If I cried, he threatened to beat me more. It seemed that all he wanted to do was to take the belt to me whenever he felt like it. But there was something my father did that hurt me more than he will ever know. My father didn't think that teenage girls should eat very *much. He called me a garbage can on more than one occasion. What is more interesting is that when I look at photographs of me as a teenager, I was nowhere near fat. However, I am now.*

I am fully aware that my father was disinterested in me. He always made me feel unimportant. As a result, I have continually chosen men who see me the same way. My interactions with my father were always negative and I seem to seek out interaction with men that are likely to have the same outcome. Until recently, they have all involved fear, punishment, adultery and emotional unavailability. My feelings have never been a priority, not to my father and not to the men in my life. I have been married and divorced three times.

"Daddy, you have had a huge impact on me. More than anything else, I have wanted you to notice the good in me and accept me for who I am. I wish I could tell you how truly awful and unjust you were to me, but it would only make you feel bad. For years, I asked myself why you treated me the way that you did. I am no longer interested in the answers. Mostly, I just want to forgive you".

Alexa, 22 years old
My father was physically and verbally abusive to me. I was scared of him, so I never spoke to him. I am always choosing men who are just like my father.

Jenna, 24 years old
When I was younger, my relationship with my father was explosive. I would do things to myself just to hurt him. I had sex at a very early age. In fact, I was always looking for love through sex. My most difficult relationship was to a boy that reminded me of my father. He was physically abusive and insulting. It ended when he tried to break my neck. I think I have always dated bad guys because of how my father treated me. "What's wrong with me, Daddy? Why don't you love me?"

SHARI R. JONAS

Wilma, 53 years old

My father was a rage-aholic. He wouldn't think twice about beating me. The funny thing is that he only hit me when he was sober. My dad was a funny, loving, weekend drunk. But a pleasant drunk. Sometimes, I wanted to be with him. We'd go to lunch and he'd tell jokes and we'd laugh. But, I never knew what I would say or do that would set him off. Therefore, I was very confused.

Despite his rage, he had a very big heart. While he would beat me for god-knows-what, he'd protect me from anything. One of my negative memories of my father was of him running after me and punching me in the back really hard. What I disliked most about him was his control.

He did change over the years. He mellowed with age. He became more relaxed, more gentle and more humourous. I'm different from my father in that I am less stubborn and less controlling.

I dated a man who reminded me of my father. He had a bad temper and was also controlling.

My ex-husband was my most difficult relationship because he abused me.

My present husband is different from my father in that he is gentle, reassuring and compromising. I can be myself with him without wondering if he might change abruptly and hurt the children or me.

As a result of my parents' marriage, I made up my mind to be the opposite. I stuck to that and although we've had ups and downs, there have been no tragedies. When I think about my father, I feel love for him. In the end, we had a great adult relationship. I wish he were here.

When Daddies Frighten

Arlene, 48 years old

As a child, I feared my father. He was impossible to predict. He would get angry easily and I stayed away when I could. Even when he would do something nice, he would yell at me. He really didn't know me at all and he made no effort to. As I grew older, he became uncomfortable with my maturation. He didn't want me to stop being a girl. He also didn't trust my judgment, though he had no reason to mistrust me.

What I disliked most about my father was his anger and the fear he seemed to provoke in my mom. He had this attitude that only what he thought and felt was of any value. He would spank with a belt and he would spank often. Usually I had no idea why I was being spanked, so it was just cruelty to me.

My most negative memory of my father occurred when I was thirteen or fourteen years old. He caught a glimpse of me changing clothes and noticed that my breasts were of different sizes. He asked me questions and demanded to take another look. Then he took me to the doctor and had the doctor look at them and ask me questions. I was humiliated and felt violated.

I remember a Father/Daughter banquet at church. I was looking forward to it. But then, dad invited another girl to join us, since her dad wouldn't attend. It was a good thing to do, but he was the wrong one to do it. The message to me was that I was not a sufficient daughter. This type of thing happened on several occasions with different girls.

There are some traits I have in common with my father. We have the same thinking patterns. We are both analytical and goal-oriented with similar problem-solving and assessment skills. Neither of us runs with the herd.

We are different though, in that he never seemed to know how to have fun and I do. He wasn't very affectionate with his children but I am very much so with mine. I am tolerant of other peoples' perspectives and ways of doing things. He never was.

Sometimes, on a Saturday, I would drive with my dad or take the train with him to his work. During that time, we would talk and share. He seemed relaxed, like he didn't have to be in charge and could be himself with me. Once there, the women in his office gave me a lot of attention. He would take me out to lunch and I could order a soda.

As I've gotten older, he's changed. He has become kinder and gentler. I can talk to him now. He is slightly more accepting of how I do things now than when he did them in the past.

My only serious romantic relationship has been with my husband, who has similar characteristics to my father. They both have excellent minds and are capable of doing many things. Both are knowledgeable and are concerned with meeting the needs of others. What makes my marriage successful is that we have mutual respect, shared values, good sense of humor and we're committed to one another.

As a result of how my father treated me, I am always seeking approval, while I am sure that I am not worthy of it. I value myself based on how other significant males see me. I have two brothers. Although they had awkward relationships with Dad, he seemed to welcome them and know what to do with them. He himself was one of six boys in his family. He would teach my brothers things about household repairs, etc. To seek my father's approval, I tried to be like my brothers. It didn't work. But to this day, I have a tendency to act like one of the guys, instead of a woman working with the guys.

"Daddy, although you were a better father to me than many of my friends had, there were things that you did that hurt me deeply, distorted some of my attitudes and limited my ability to function. I'm sure that you never intended any of what you did to be hurtful, but I wonder if you ever thought for a minute about how I might have felt or reacted in the situations you arranged. In many ways you were very thoughtless and careless with me. I know now that you were doing the best you could with what you had, given your upbringing and the culture at the time."

Heidi, 29 years old

Dad was always the disciplinarian, always pushing me to study, never approving of boyfriends. Actually, I was quite scared of him. What I dislike most about him was how intimidating he could be. My most negative memory was of him shouting at me, then slapping me because I had not cooked his dinner properly. I'm different from my father in that I am very physically affectionate and less confident in personal relationships.

There is a definitely a pattern as a result of how my father treated me. For a long time, I saw any sign of physical affection as indicating a deep love and caring. Therefore, I allowed myself to become involved in physical relationships when I did not want sex just because the physical contact made me feel loved.

When I think about my father, I feel love, anger and sadness. "Dad, I wish you had cuddled me as a little girl. I have done some stupid things, but I have done well. I wish I could have had you as a confidante. However, I am glad that we have grown closer over the years and I love you very much."

Annie, 27 years old

My father was a perfectionist, nit-picky and anal-retentive. He was also a social and cultural snob. We weren't very close. He was away a lot and when he was around, he wasn't very warm. Most of the time, I feared him. I always felt as if I never measured up to his standards. I felt very defective. It seemed as if he was forever criticizing me about something, even the slightest action. I remember him criticizing the fact that I had a weak grip while holding my silverware or toothbrush. I have always made sure that I dated only men who were not neat or orderly. I am a total sucker for compliments, since my father never gave me any. On the other hand, I refused to date anyone who was culturally ignorant. Every one was somewhat snobby or elitist. In that way, I looked up to my father. However, I'm not proud of this.

"Daddy, the thought of speaking to you frightens me. I'm sorry that our relationship is not where I hoped it would be. I would love to feel closer to you, but I'm afraid of making the first move for fear of being criticized. My deepest fear is that you would die and I would end up feeling incomplete for the rest of my life. I would always blame myself for not making enough of an effort to bridge the gap between us."

Kelly, 14 years old

I don't like my father. He's a hypocrite and has very bad mood swings. He can be nice and funny, but I'm scared of him. Most of the time we're okay, but I do wish we were closer. What I dislike most about my father is his terrible mood swings and that he is prejudiced. He always yells at me for hanging out with black guys. With my first black boyfriend, he almost disowned me. He didn't talk to me for one month, which was the best month of my life. He swears that I do things just to spite him.

I have had a few boyfriends who had mood swings and who yelled a lot. One boyfriend was different from my father. He was open to new experiences, listened to my point of view and was very sweet. We both understood each other. He listened, he talked and he promised to take everything slowly. He tried the hardest not to flip out on me.

As a result of how my father treats me, I'm very scared to get close to a guy. If I get the slightest idea that they don't like me, I'll break up with them. If they're very controlling, I get scared and will just listen and agree with everything they say.

Thinking about my father gets me really mad and then I want to cry. " I lost all respect for you when I was twelve years old. No matter what you want to believe, I will always feel the way I do. I can't believe that you cannot accept me for me. You should know that you've ruined any chance of me having a good relationship and trusting anyone. Isn't that pathetic?"

Rose, 42 years old

Early in our relationship, I worshipped my father. As I aged, our relationship became terribly strained. I feared him and still do to this day. My father is an unreasonable, mean-spirited man who degrades his children and anyone else who doesn't live up to his standards. My most negative memory of my father is sitting at the dinner table, not wanting to say anything for fear of causing an argument or upsetting him. I used to rip my paper napkin into tiny pieces during every meal. What I dislike most about him was his constant complaining and yelling about how we weren't doing our best or we weren't working hard enough. Our worth was wrapped up in what we accomplished. It was total conditional love. He never said anything positive to us.

My ex-husband reminded me of my father. He was a perfectionist, compulsive alcoholic. He committed first degree murder and is currently serving a twenty-seven year sentence. He became more and more needy of my depleting emotional stability.

As a result of always seeking my father's approval in everything I did, I've looked for the same approval with every man I've been with. Most of them were perfectionists, too. I molded myself into what they wanted, hiding my true self. Getting others' approval by any means necessary is a serious problem in my life, to this day. I am constantly looking for pats on the back.

When I think about my father, I feel fear and anger. "I hope you can mellow out and live life the way it is and not for what you expect it to be. Stop being so judgmental and learn to laugh at yourself. Lighten up on the critical outlook. Be more positive."

Jillian, 21 years old

When I was young, my father was a miserable, mean, strict, stubborn and irrational man. Everyone in the house feared him, including the dog. He and I fought constantly. I have always been the one to say what everyone was thinking. So, I often suffered my father's wrath. We had good times though. He and I always enjoyed nature walks and bird spotting. But, he always managed to spoil a wonderful family occasion with some comment or fight.

My most negative memory of my father occurred when I was seventeen years old. My father had just come home from work and I was watching the end of a movie. I had previously cleaned the house (so that he would have nothing to complain about) but my little brother had made a mess in the kitchen that I didn't know about. My father sees it and asks me to clean it up and not very nicely. I ask him if I can watch the last five minutes of the movie first. The situation quickly escalated to a physical fight. The tension had been thick between us for about a year. After a scuffle, I ran outside where he chased and caught me. He threw me in my room. But, I jumped out the window and went to my friend's house where I stayed for a couple of days.

Presently, my boyfriend of three years is completely opposite to my father. He is sensitive to my feelings and needs and accepts me and my decisions without question. I love him. I've never been in love before him. I never took any other guy I dated seriously. I cheated on every single one of them, even the three or four significant ones. I did so without a thought. I never let anyone get to know the real me inside. My present relationship is about love, trust, openness and knowing each other's every thought.

As a result of my relationship with my father, I have always feared men and kept my relationships light. I cheated so that they could not hurt me first. I also love attention from men, probably because I always wanted it from him when I was young. When I became sexually active at age nineteen, I chose men who were emotionally unavailable. None of them treated me right or gave me the respect I deserved. Thank God I met my boyfriend when I did.

When I think about my father, I feel sadness, love and pity. "Daddy, I love you very much. I just want you to be proud of me, of who I really am and not who you'd like me to be. I am very grateful for all you have given me. I just wish we could get along better."

Marlene, 44 years old

My father wasn't physically abusive, but I was afraid of him. He was mean. He didn't like me. I couldn't do anything right in his eyes. He never listened. It was his way or no way. He was a firm believer that kids should be seen and not heard. My first husband was very much like my father in his personality; opinionated, intolerant of others, self-righteous and when he was drunk he became verbally and physically abusive. I married him just to get out of my house. I think I was looking for a man like my father who would approve of me and give me the love I so desperately wanted as a child. My current husband is completely opposite to my father and my ex. He is a recovering alcoholic and has been sober for almost ten years. He is calm, relaxed, passive, very loving and very caring.

"Daddy, why didn't you like me? Why did you treat me that way? I am so angry with you because we never had the father/daughter relationship that I've always wanted. Now, it's too late."

Sharon, 21 years old

My father was very abusive, very controlling and completely unpredictable. He could be laughing one minute and hitting me for tracking mud into the house the next. No one was ever sure what would please him or what would set him off. He verbally, emotionally, physically and sexually abused me and I believe my brother. I was terrified of my father. I lived in a constant state of fear. His rules could change at any minute. No matter what I did, I couldn't keep my brother or myself safe. I have dissociative identity disorder; a multiple self system. Some loved him, while others hated him completely. Some never came out when he was around, while others have no memory of him. He was a very demanding person. We were expected to meet his every need. I spent a lot of time trying to anticipate his needs and wants to avoid getting punished. Even at his best, there was an undercurrent that could explode at any minute. Whenever I meet someone who reminds me of my father, I become physically ill. So, I only date people (men and women) who are opposite to my father in varying degrees. I have spent my whole life defending myself against my father. At present, he doesn't know where I live or how to reach me. I visit him a few times a year and on my terms. People always seems to react in shock when I tell them that my father can live, die, get sick or move to Mars and it wouldn't make a difference to my life, except that I would have one less person to be afraid of.

Tricia, 42 years old

I was afraid of my father. He was a tyrant. He was cruel, scary, mean-spirited and explosive. He physically abused my mother and psychologically abused me. During my parents divorce, my father made several attempts to kill my mother. He managed to kidnap her on several occasions. During their marriage, he committed adultery several times. He was a flashy dresser and a good dancer. My first husband looked like my father, always wanted everything his way and was very psychologically abusive. Most of the guys I dated looked like my father; tall, dark and handsome. Finally, I married a man who is the complete opposite of my father. He is shy, passive, more feminine and less ambitious. He has a different overall body type and coloring, too. In this relationship, I run the show. He goes along with all my plans and doesn't tell me what to do. "Daddy, did you ever love me? Why did you terrorize me all the time? When I was crying and you'd say, 'Shut up or I'll give you something to cry about' how come you couldn't see that I already had a reason? I feel sorry for your miserable life."

Courtney, 28 years old

I was always afraid of my father. He was very strict, stubborn and could easily lose control. I'll never forget one Sunday when I was in church. The songbook fell from my hands and in order to avoid it hitting the floor and making a noise, I grabbed a page, causing it to tear out. My father saw me stick the page in my pocket and he gave me that "you're in trouble" look. When we got home, he used a razor strap to beat me. He lost control of his temper and hit me in the face, leaving a two inch welt. He made me tell everyone that I fell on the sidewalk. I seem to pick controlling men who believe that a man should do the thinking and the woman does as she is told.

"Dad, parents aren't given instruction manuals. I know that you raised me the best way you knew how. I don't think that you hurt me or abused me on purpose. I don't hold anything against you, but I do have problems because of some of the things that happened and I want you to remember that. I love you, anyway."

Wendy, 22 years old

My father always controlled my mother. She did everything he said and agreed with everything he did until the day he walked through the door and told her that he didn't love her anymore.

I would describe my father as very loving, up until I was the age of twelve. Then he became very controlling and insensitive. He was the type to make you feel like you were nothing. By the time I was thirteen years old, my father and I never spoke unless it was necessary. I didn't like the person that he was and I don't think that he liked the person that I was at the time. He put me down a lot. He had a hard time accepting me and I had a hard time dealing with that. I was a very sensitive person and he was very overbearing. We didn't get along for many years. What I disliked most about my father is that he always put me down if I didn't do things the way he wanted me to.

My most difficult relationship was with someone who was verbally abusive and controlling. He put me down often and made me feel worthless. It finally ended when I told him that I was pregnant. He said that he was going away and that he'd send baby postcards telling it to rape and kill me. Then he'd laugh. I aborted the baby and never talked to him again.

My most successful relationship is with my fiance. We understand and accept each other for the way that we are. We don't try to change each other. We are both loving and supportive

SHARI R. JONAS

toward one another and we trust each other.

As a result of my relationship with my father, I think that I have always gravitated toward controlling people, people with stronger personalities than me. People who made me feel hatred toward myself and toward life in general. But, I think that I overcame that in the end.

When I think of my father, I feel anger, frustration and sadness. "I love you because you're my father, but I hate all the things that you put me through. I hate you for making me feel like I will never be good enough for you. I hate you for setting a standard that I will probably never reach and I hate you for leaving Mommy and me and then putting me in the middle of it."

When Daddies Rule

Debbie, 21 years old
My father is a very controlling man. He was never physically abusive, only verbally. He would put on a show in front of people that made it look like he and my mom got along, but they didn't. Mom just filed for divorce. She's sick of being treated like crap.

My father was always busy with his job. When he would get home from work, he expected his dinner to be ready at 5:30. He expected that since he was the male, he ruled the roost. What I disliked most about him was how he always had to have things in the household his way. I'm different from my dad. For one, I don't believe that a man rules the household.

Recently, he has gone through a mid-life crisis, which consisted of taking early retirement, having an affair and purchasing a sports car.

I was always afraid of him. Once he got so mad at me for waking him when I slammed a door, that he threw me down on the ground.

I always went to Mom when I had a problem. I hated when she would make me take a ride with him. I just didn't like him. For a long time, I didn't call him Dad. He was "Steve."

What I loved most about him was he was my father. He gave me a sense of family.

One boyfriend reminded me of my father. He was controlling, made me feel inferior. He tried to make me out to be the stupid one. It was my mother who made me aware that he was just like my father. For a while, I thought it was okay to be dominated. Then I broke free and went away to college. I've since learned that a woman has just as many rights as a man and doesn't have to be controlled.

When I think of my father, I feel disgust and disapproval. I feel sorry for my mother for putting up with him for twenty-eight years.

"Dad, you've treated my mother like crap for so long. I disrespect you more than you could possibly know for that. You thought that you kept everything hidden from my brother and me. But the older we got, the more we saw. You think that just because you are a man and because your father was in charge of your household, that's the way it's going to be for you. Well, times have changed and women no longer have to put up with shit like that anymore."

Robin, 35 years old

My father's main role in the family seemed to be that of "enforcer." To outsiders, he was very outgoing and extremely funny. To me, he was very controlling and easily disappointed. When I was younger, my relationship with my father was strained, at best. I never felt as if I knew him or that he knew me. I was hungry for his approval. When that didn't seem forthcoming, I went to the other extreme and did things I knew he would not approve of.

What I disliked most about my father is that he was a bigot and very critical. Even now, when I watch reruns of "All in the Family", I see Archie Bunker and am transported back to my childhood.

I'm like my father in that I find myself to be overly critical, at times. I have to make an effort to be affectionate. I also have

SHARI R. JONAS

a great sense of humor like he has. I'm very different from my father in that I am an avid learner. I love to learn about everything from art to brain surgery. While my father is not a stupid man, his intelligence about anything other than common sense is limited. I also read quite a bit, something he never did. I do think I am more compassionate than he is.

My husband is completely opposite to my father. He is extremely affectionate. He comes from a very close-knit family, although they have a few skeletons of their own. Where my father seemed to be either hot or cold, my husband is always warm. My husband is rarely moody and is not afraid to take responsibility for his own actions and words. My dad never did or said anything that was not a direct result of something someone else did or said.

What makes my marriage so successful is that my husband and I were not children when we married. We knew what we were getting involved in when we took on the responsibility of a family. Unlike my parents who were just sixteen when they married and only seventeen when I was born. Also, I have learned what personality traits I could tolerate in another person. I have been very honest with my husband about my family dynamics and so he really understands me when I appear to over react to something he's done or said.

The only marriage I have ever witnessed was that of my parents. Seeing as that kind of life never appealed to me, I never let any other relationships ever mature to the point that it would be considered serious — until I met my husband. Even then, my husband and I lived together for more than a year before I agreed to get married. By that time, I had a taste of what my own married life would be like and figured it wouldn't be so bad.

As a result of how my father treated me, I found myself screaming away from any man that resembled my father in any way. When I think about my father I feel many emotions. Guilt, because I feel bad saying negative things about someone I love. Regret, because I wish it could have been different. Anger, because I see my younger sister is still caught in the web of trying to please a man that she will never please. Love, because in spite of everything, he is my father and I love him. I think he loves me too, as much as he is capable of. And understanding, because although I am one of those who hate it when people try to blame their own failings on things that happen to them, I do understand some of the reasons he was the way he was. I think that maybe, he did the best he could with what he had to work with, the tools his own parents give him to use and all the knowledge that a seventeen-year-old child possesses about raising a family.

"Daddy, did I ever make you proud? Please tell me if I did."

Karen, 40 years old

I only had my Dad in my life for the first eighteen years, at which point he died of a heart attack at the age of forty-five. My father came from a home where his dad was physically abusive towards his mother. We were lucky that he didn't turn out that way. But, growing up in a home like he had did leave him with scars.

It wasn't until I got into my teens that I realized that things weren't all they should be. Dad was very controlling and jealous and they didn't have friends. My father wouldn't allow my mother to work. I remember my parents fighting a lot, but I don't remember about what. I don't know if I blocked that out because I always tried to ignore it or turn up the radio so I wouldn't hear it. My mother knew exactly how to push my Dad's buttons and took full advantage of it at times. As far as I know he didn't hit her. I never saw any bruises. I think he just controlled her with the money and by not making transportation a priority for her. Often times, my mother was stuck at home because she didn't have a car. There was a period of about eight years when we didn't even have a phone.

As a young girl, my daddy was both fun and scary. If everyone was behaving themselves and his work was going well, all was right with the world. But if any of us were misbehaving or the job situation was stressful — watch out! Mom took care of most of the discipline, but when Dad spanked you, it was dead *serious. It wasn't abuse in my mind. And it was rare, because we were pretty well-behaved. They put the fear of God into us and we remembered.*

Dad watched cartoons with us every Saturday morning and enjoyed them as much as we did. My memories of him between the ages of five and fifteen are mostly of a smiling, laughing person.

I was the only girl out of four kids. So, I was kind of a strange thing that my dad didn't know how to handle. He hadn't had any sisters either, so a little girl was a whole new world to him. I always felt that the boys were closer to him. They would do guy stuff and I wasn't a part of it. I felt left out. But, there were times when he would make sure I was included.

Once I became a teenager, he grew more distant. I think my becoming a sexual being made him really uncomfortable. I also became very involved in the school band and I put everything into that. I really felt that by the time I got into Junior High school, there really wasn't much of a relationship with my dad. He worked seven days a week and very long hours when the weather cooperated. So, he just wasn't around that much. But when he was there, we'd still have those same Saturday morning cartoon times.

I'm like my dad in that I need to be in control of most things in my life. I'd rather be the one driving the car. I'd rather have a pile of work on my desk that requires me to come in and work all weekend than delegate it out to someone else just because I want to be in control. It's a bit of a struggle.

My brothers are all damaged goods in different ways because of the environment we grew up in. I think I was able to adjust better to life as a result of not being involved so closely with my father.

My dad weighed about three-hundred and fifty pounds most of my teen years. He weighed over four hundred pounds the year before he died. I really hated the fact the he had let himself get so overweight. It was embarrassing for me on the rare occasions when we'd be out somewhere and my schoolmates

*could see that he was my dad. He really lacked self-discipline. He
was pretty strict with discipline on us, but had none for himself.*

*The man I married is completely opposite to my father. He
values education, is interested in physical fitness, has a relationship with his own parents, respects authority and has a balanced
relationship with his sons and his daughter.*

*I didn't date at all until after Dad died, when I was
eighteen years old. Then I spent the entire year looking desperately
for that masculine attention I was craving. As is usually the case,
the attention I got wasn't the right kind. I was looking for someone to love me, but I was settling for one-nighters. I met my
husband just before I turned twenty. Our relationship took off
like a rocket. I got lucky in that he filled every need that I had
for that love that I'd been looking for.*

*When I think about my father, I get very sad. Sad, because
I never really knew him when I had him. Sad, because from what
my mom has told me about their marriage, I don't think I would
have liked him very much, having understood the way he treated
her. I loved him, but at the same time, I'm glad that I don't have
to deal with it anymore.*

*"I love you Daddy and I just hope that I've made you
proud. I hope that you'll always know how much I appreciated
all that you tried to do for our family. I know it was the best way
you knew how."*

Carrie, 25 years old

*My father was hardly ever around. When he was, he was very
intimidating. We weren't close at all. My parents divorced when
I was twelve years old. Up until that time, my father made all of
the decisions in my life. I was never allowed to have an opinion.
After the divorce, I moved out of state with my mom. The first
year my father sent me a teddy bear, which I thought was
inappropriate for my age. That was the first and last gift I ever
received from him. We have since lost complete contact.*

*My most negative memory of my father was when he sent
me out in the dark to buy him a soda. I didn't want to go*

because I was afraid of the dark. He made me. When I was coming back, he was waiting outside. He scared me so bad, I pissed in my panties.

I'm different from my father. I take care of my responsibilities and I'm an honest person.

My first husband was like my father. He was self-centered and lacked communication skills. He too, would steal from his own family. He was very controlling and would often lie to me. It finally ended when I found out he was sleeping with my best friend.

My current husband is completely opposite to my father. He is very family oriented, very good at communicating and would do anything for me. He takes the time to find out what is wrong when I'm upset. He listens when I have a problem and he puts forth a real effort to make things better when things are going well.

As a result of my relationship with my father, I married my first husband, a very controlling man who never considered what I wanted.

When I think about my father, I feel sadness and anger. I never want him to come back.

When Daddies Scar

Brittany, 18 years old

My father never hit me. But, I have been emotionally and verbally abused by him. He was a violent man, always yelling, hitting and throwing things. Although my parents got divorced two years ago, he still verbally abuses my mother whenever they speak.

My father and I never had a real relationship with true feelings and conversation. He never understood me. I dislike everything about my father, especially his violent temper. Once, I asked him to be a little quieter so that I could hear the TV. He kicked a chair, then threw a book at me.

My father has gotten worse. He smokes, drinks and swears all the time. He is also very depressed. Before my parents were divorced, he cheated on my mother. Now, his ex-girlfriend is pregnant.

My ex-boyfriend reminded me of my father. He was rude, selfish and stubborn. The relationship ended when he cheated on me and told me about it.

I'm different than my father in that I am understanding and caring about others. But, when I get mad, I do yell. I also have this violent urge to yell, even when something very little goes wrong.

As a result of my relationship with my father, I always need to feel very secure and I have to be the only one. I need to be the center of attention and I always need to be held and told how much I am loved. When I think about my father, I feel anger and mistrust. There isn't anything I could say to my father, because he never listens. Even if he would be receptive, he would never understand me.

Kim, 20 years old

I have always been scared of my father. He never hurt us physically, but emotionally he tore us apart. I never remember feeling comfortable around him. I love him and he loves me, but we really don't like each other. He favors my sister over everyone else and he treats my mom like garbage.

One of my boyfriends reminded me of my father. He was rough with people, he had that asshole demeanor and I was scared of him. He was physically, emotionally and mentally abusive to me for ten months and three days. It took me a year and a half of therapy and I still have nightmares. Now, I am a volunteer at a battered women's shelter.

As a result of my relationship with my father, I am attracted to guys that are either jerks like him or too gentle and passive.

When I think about my father, I feel anger, resentment, pity (for him and me) and sadness. It doesn't have to be like this. "F— you, Daddy. You hurt me and disappointed me more than you will ever know. But, I still love you."

S H A R I   R.   J O N A S

Noreen, 46 years old

My father was a tyrant. He was scary, mean-spirited and explosive at times. I was afraid of him. While my parents were married, there was a lot of verbal fighting and occasional physical conflict. My father committed adultery on several occasions. My dad wanted to control everything and be the boss. During their divorce, my father tried to kill my mother a couple of times. My father died of cancer at the age of fifty-one and my mother is happily remarried.

My most negative memory of my father is when he physically abused my mother. What I disliked most about him was his psychological abuse towards my sister, my mother and myself.

My first husband reminded me of my father. He looked like him. He always wanted things his way and he was psychologically abusive. I couldn't take it anymore and I divorced him.

My present husband is completely opposite to my father. He is shy, passive, has more feminine qualities and is less ambitious. Even his body type and coloring is different. In this relationship, I run the show. He doesn't tell me what to do.

As a result of my relationship with my father, I married a man who also psychologically abused me. In fact, most of the guys I dated looked like my father; tall, dark and handsome.

When I think about my father I feel anger, pity and sadness. "Why did you always force, threat or bark orders at me to get me to do things? Why did you terrorize me all the time? Did you ever love me? When I was crying and you said, "Shut up or I'll give you something to cry about, how come you couldn't see that I already had something to cry about? I feel sorry for your miserable life."

Sheila, 31 years old

My Dad was an emotionally abusive bully. His psychological punishments were for his own amusement. It was horrible. We never knew what was going to set him off. I still have a hard time thinking about it. The last time he hit me I was 26 years old and already a physician. It was a very difficult moment. I felt so small, so betrayed and indignant. It seemed as if it wasn't happening to me, that I was outside myself watching this strange scene unfold.

Ironically, as a young child, I thought I was so lucky to have him as my dad. As a teenager, he was so protective and controlling (not in the normal way). As a young adult, a lot began to resurface. Once I graduated and became a doctor, just like him, I figured that now we were peers. I was wrong. It made everything worse. I think that on some level, I became the enemy. He told my siblings that he doesn't like me. I haven't been able to trace what it was that caused the turning point.

I have dated men who remind me of my father. I seem to enjoy men who feel they need to dominate me. I seem to enjoy the struggle for independence. I enjoy the ritual of the argument.

One of my most difficult relationships started out as a friendship.

I fought the closeness and treated him awfully. He was completely opposite to my father. In this one, I was the one who was psychologically abusive. After a couple of years, I realized that I really loved him. It was too late. It became his turn to pay me back for all the crappy things I did and said. Eventually, we drove each other to complete misery. I regret it now. It finally ended when I met someone else and true to form I rubbed it in his face. I verbally tormented him one night, until he was reduced to tears. We haven't spoken in over a year.

As a result of my relationship with my father, I like to dominate the men in my life. Whenever I meet the dominating type, I enjoy arguing with them. It's as if the script is being replayed, word for word. I don't like to admit this, but I enjoy knocking men down to size. When I think about my father, I feel resentment. He's really a jerk. He fashioned himself as some kind of sage and he knows I no longer buy into it.

Alyssa, 21 years old

As a young child, I thought my father was the best man in the world. We had our fights, but he assured me that I was his favorite. I was only concerned with pleasing him and yet, he constantly hurt me emotionally, especially in the later years of our relationship. One night, he made me sit on the floor of the basement while he looked down at me from his chair and called me a slut, whore and many other colorful phrases. I was sixteen years old. Another time, I won the Girl of the Year award at my junior high graduation for my grades, school activities and community contributions. My father told me that he did all the work for that award and I did nothing. I asked for clarification, but he remained adamant. My grades didn't stay up after that and my activities decreased as well.

What I dislike most about my father was his abusive temper and his lying manipulations. He also tried to drive a wedge between my mother, my sisters and myself, in order to make himself look and feel good.

As an adult, he treats me worse than ever before because I have chosen my own path, rather then the one he wanted for me. He uses my sister to do this. I think he's losing his grip on reality or he's just getting worse at lying.

My ex-boyfriend reminded me of my father. He also had a horrible mean streak and an abusive nature. He was emotionally, verbally, physically and sexually abusive. He even told my friend that he was seeing how much he could mess with my mind. My father and him hated each other because they both fought for control over me. In the end, he raped me and I realized that he did not love me. I knew that the only way that all the pain would stop would be if I got myself together and left him.

Thank God I did.

My husband was one of the first men that came into my life after a long line of abusive men all of whom were like my *father. Other than the fact that my husband and my father are both intelligent, they are polar opposites. My husband is gentle, loving, honest, compassionate and cares about my feelings and goals. My achievements are my own and he supports whatever endeavor I choose. He has helped me to understand my father.*

I have always dated men that reminded me of my father. I was playing out the same patterns of trying to please them. The outcomes were always abusive and awful. I finally realized that that was not what I wanted.

When I think about my father, I feel hatred, rage and sadness. Sometimes, I still ache for his approval, which I know I will never have and is not worth the effort.

"Daddy, I don't think I could ever forgive you for what you did to me. I don't know how you sleep at night. I want you to know that I hate myself for loving you and I work against it every day. Sad, isn't it?"

Dahlia, 20 years old

My father was never a father nor a husband. He was always looking for faults in all of us so that he could abuse us, physically and mentally. He would spit in mum's face, telling her that she was repulsive, hitting her, threatening her. We were all referred to as, "You, from your mum's vagina." He's a mean, cold, hard, cruel and heartless man. I wish that I was never born to him. If only my father was different. I don't have one particular negative memory of my father. It's been just about every day of my life spent in his presence, which is why I left home when I was fourteen.

Thanks to my father, I am very wary of men. If I see any characteristics in me that might be similar to him, then I change. When searching for a partner, I search for someone very opposite to my father.

When I think about him, I feel tied up, repressed, with a heavy feeling in my chest. Sometimes I feel sad, but I try not to be. That is the harsh reality of life.

"I wish you'd realize what you've done and apologize. Why can't you ever change?"

Louise, 44 years old

When I was between five and ten years of age, I thought my father was wonderful. He was someone to look up to. But from ten to fifteen years of age, things went from good to bad. The best word to describe him was absent. He was too busy to spend time with his children. He wouldn't come to see us on a regular basis and he didn't pay child support. He was always making excuses. My father's priorities revolved around himself and what he wanted. He became a womanizer, always trying to conquer younger women. He certainly was not a father figure. Eventually, I grew to resent him.

I have several really negative memories of my father. Spanking me with his gun belt, lying that he was coming to get us for a weekend or a vacation and never paying his fair share of our upbringing, just to name a few.

He was not there as a father in any capacity and spent all of his time and affection on his new step-family. He expected me to go to a grand university and when I chose a different plan, he was angry and disappointed with me.

He was very vocal about the fact that I didn't finish school and measure up to his expectations. Yet, he didn't get past the tenth grade.

I'm very different from my father. To me, family comes first. I am compassionate and have concerns for other peoples' feelings. Even if I don't agree, I still value their opinions. According to my father, if you don't agree with his ideas, then you're nothing to him. He refuses to meet anyone half way on anything. I, on the other hand, will try to make a relationship work.

My priorities in life are to watch my adult children continue to grow and to support their needs. Also, to spend my non-working hours with my husband, sharing the life we've built together. I feel that it's okay to be me and have the desires in life that I have.

My ex-husband reminded me of my father. He was opinionated, driven, domineering, bitter, aggressive and unsupportive of my opinions and thoughts. He was mentally and physically abusive. Nothing was ever good enough and he was constantly belittling people.

My present husband is completely opposite to my father. He is shy, thoughtful of others' feelings, supportive and respectful. He has morals and values and respects women for something other than their bodies. What makes our marriage successful is that we are able to counterbalance each other's personality. We both realize that any relationship is a full time job. We don't "sweat the small stuff." We nurture each other's thoughts and value each other as friends and partners — even the sexual portion of our relationship.

Thanks to my father, I found myself always attracted to men who were either aloof with their feelings and affections or who were aggressive and abusive.

When I think about my father, I feel anger and sorrow. I feel sorry for him and for the way his life has turned out. He has alienated his children. Furthermore, he is not willing to change.

"Daddy, I love you, regardless of what you've done. I know that you didn't have a positive role-model attitude. I just want you to accept me for the way I am and be proud of my accomplishments in life."

When Daddies Touch

To read the stories of fathers who sexually abused their daughters and not experience every range of negative human emotion is virtually impossible. I felt sadness and sorrow, nausea and disgust, anger and outrage. I wanted to save every little girl and reprimand every depraved father. With each story, I'd shake my head and ask the question that we all ask when we hear of the unspeakable, "Who could do such a thing?" It is clear to me now why child molesters are not safe in prison. Even hardened criminals are disgusted by such despicable behavior. Though I am a professional and should refrain from passing judgment, I am both a parent and a woman and so I say this with a clear conscious: Of all

SHARI R. JONAS

the fathers in the world, none are worse than those who have inappropriately touched their little girls.

We should have pity on them, for they are obviously very disturbed humans and very wounded souls. What other reasonable explanation can we surmise to account for such wrongful behavior? The notion becomes even more disturbing when you realize that the adult touching the child is also the father. Shouldn't he know better? We expect a parent to protect their own child, but when that parent is ill, all systems fail. As a result, these children and adult survivors who become emotionally maimed need more nurturing, more love and more kindness than most people require in a lifetime. Is it any wonder they have difficulty in establishing trust and building relationships with all other men in their lives?

If you are a survivor of incest, you can heal. Although you feel alone, you are not. There are many women like yourself who are ready and willing to assist you in your recovery process. Take your time, but do the work. The results will revive your spirit, give meaning to your life and enable you to experience the joys of a relationship.

If you are not a survivor, thank your lucky stars and pray as hard as you can that the prevalence of incest diminishes with each passing day. All the while, let us keep our eyes and ears open to the sights and sounds of little children everywhere who might be holding the deepest, cruelest secret in the world.

Leslie, 22 years old

I hate my father. He is a slimy, child-molesting jerk. As a child, I did everything I could to get away from him. I hope, even today, to never have to see him again.

When I was four my parents got divorced. My younger brother and I would go to visit my dad every other weekend. At age fourteen, I stopped because he was molesting me. At sixteen, my brother stopped, because my dad stole a bunch of money from him.

Basically, my relationship with my father was sexual. My worst memory of him was when I was eight, he tried to have anal sex with me. My most positive memory of my father was when I was sixteen. I got into some trouble. Dad made me lie across a coffee table to beat me with his belt. Then, he told me that I was his bright, shining star and he wanted me to go far in life.

I'm different from my dad in that I have respect for myself and for others. I am not concerned with getting drunk every night and riding around on my motorcycle. I can have a conversation with someone and never use the word "I". His priorities have always been himself. My priorities are to raise my son on my own and have him be a good man. Further-more, I want to support myself and never rely on a man to take care of me.

I have never gotten seriously involved with anyone that remotely reminded me of my father because I refuse to date someone that filthy. However, there was someone who I went on two dates with. He was insecure, self-absorbed and completely unable to relate to people. I realized that I would eventually despise this man and broke it off fast.

I am involved with someone right now who has many opposing characteristics to my father. His only concern is me, to the point that he loses himself. He's never stingy or selfish. He never touches me when I don't want him to. He respects me, my space and my needs. He spoils me rotten and really does care for me.

A short while ago, I tried to break up with him. (It didn't work, so I gave up trying for now.) I really don't want to be in a relationship at all. I discovered that I am co-dependent. I want to be alone to find out how strong I can be. I want to depend on me for a while. I also do not believe that there is one person for everyone. I find that I can enjoy my time with who I am without worrying about marriage and all that "relationship" stuff.

When I think about my father, I feel anger, hatred, disgust, sadness and shame.

As a result of my father sexually molesting me, I use sex to make people like me. Their actual opinion of me doesn't matter, as long as I can hop into bed with them and make it all right.

SHARI R. JONAS

Phyllis, 39 years old

My father was a mean, perverted drunk. He molested me and my older sister. He started fondling me when I was around three or four years old. It didn't stop until I was in elementary school, which was during my fifth or sixth grade.

My parents' relationship was explosive. They were very unhappy and both extremely jealous of others. My father accused my mother of being unfaithful and apparently, she did have an affair. My father was physically and verbally abusive. They fought all the time. My most negative memory of my father was when he beat my mom so badly that her face was bleeding and her shirt was torn to pieces. What I dislike most about him is that he treated my mom terribly. He beat and berated her. He called her ugly names. He would also call my older sister and me dirty names.

When I was younger, I adored my father. Then I became his "special one." He always treated me like I was different, better than my sisters. Once I became a teenager and started going out on dates, our relationship became explosive. He accused me of having sex and being bad. I was. I did drugs and was sexually active by the time I was fifteen years old. He was physically and verbally abusive towards me. There were times when I wanted him to die or just go away. I even thought of ways I could kill him.

The only real, positive, memory of my father is when my daughter was about a year old, he brought her a stuffed animal because she was sick. She is now ten.

There isn't anything about my father that I love. I only have a relationship with because he is my father and I don't want my children to know that anything is wrong.

I'm like my dad in that I am a bit of a loner. I have friends, but I enjoy my solitude. I am also quite insecure in most of my relationships.

I married my husband when I was twenty years old. I was infatuated with him. He was a gorgeous, sweet alcoholic. He has been in recovery now for six years. He is no longer the sweet, easygoing guy I married because he is no longer drunk all the time. I am only realizing this since he quit drinking and his real personality has come out. He is controlling, seems to have lost his sense of humor and is almost always unhappy. We have major communication problems. I can't seem to live up to his expectations, no matter what I do. However, since I want my kids to be in a stable home environment, I am staying with him. I am doing just what my mother did — feeling financially trapped!

I only dated the good guys for a short time while I was in high school. They were nice, well-adjusted people. But, I guess I didn't feel good enough for them. So, I chose to date emotionally needy guys, ones that were bad or who had drug and alcohol problems.

When I think about my father, I feel anger, disgust and sorrow. I feel sick to my stomach when think of my childhood and just want the memories to be erased.

"Why did you pick me to be your favorite girl? I hate you for it. I have learned to distrust people and my own feelings because of what you did to me. You really screwed me up. And I really hate you for what you did to my mom. She was so sweet and so special and you hurt her so badly. Why did you hurt her? Explain that to me. Don't blame anyone else. Just tell me why you did those things. I'm ashamed of what you did to me and my sister and my mom. I can't even recall stories for my kids because most of my memories are bad ones. I want you to know that I only feel sorry for you. I feel sorry because I am ashamed of you. I will NEVER trust you with my kids."

Charlotte, 45 years old

I am the TV repairman's daughter. My parents were never married. I finally met my natural father at the age of thirty. I had sex with him. When I was ten my mother married my step-father. I had sex with him, too. I was expected to service all the men in the family. I've been divorced twice. Every relationship I ever had was abusive.

Kathryn, 34 years old

My father is a mean, degrading, emotionally abusive man who spent years sexually molesting my sisters and me. Obviously, we don't speak to him. All of my boyfriends were completely different from my father. I looked for the exact opposite of him. I chose non-abusive men. But, I have to admit that I liked men who showed me attention, affection and respect. My husband won my heart because he was (and still is) so gentle and considerate; the complete opposite of my messed-up father.

Whenever I think of my father, I'm filled with confusion. I have no idea how he could have molested, beaten and horribly degraded us. The evil in his heart baffles me. When I was younger, I was filled with anger and rage. But now, I am more confused than anything. Sometimes, I feel pity for him, sometimes I am very angry with him. Mostly, I am confused. My sisters and I have confronted our father. We said everything we needed to say. Most of all, I want an apology or at least an acknowledgement of the abuse, but that will never happen. He won't even admit to it.

Caitlin, 23 years old

My father sexually abused me. There was no love or caring when he did it. I was basically an inanimate object. He would also beat me with a belt if I didn't behave myself. I went from loving and fearing him to pretending he didn't exist.

"Dad, I should forgive you for your mistakes, but I don't. Everything I hated in you, I look for the opposite in men. You taught me what not to accept in a man, which has made me a pro in dealing with men. I love men when it seems I should hate them. You seem to have had more to do with the woman that I grew up to be than my mother did. That is both so scary and so precious at the same time."

Rhonda, 34 years old

My father was a monster. Our relationship was a sexual one.

"I hate you for what you've made of me. I hate that I cannot get my life together. It's all your fault. I am empty inside and I don't deserve this. I hope you feel guilty the way I do so that you may be in pain. I hate you, I hate you, I hate you. But, I don't wish death or harm to you, just pain. Why I cannot abandon you is beyond me. I guess even with all the shit you have done to me you are still my dad. May God have mercy on you soul."

Belinda, 28 years old

My father physically, emotionally and sexually abused me. But, he was also charming and charismatic, as well. Once my mother left, I took care of the house. So, I often viewed my father as a husband, or as a boss, or as a pal. I haven't called him dad since I was ten years old. I have dissociative identity disorder. Most of the direct abuse was done to the others inside of me, so that I didn't have to experience it. They don't have mixed feelings about him like I do, they just hate and fear him. Personally, I was out and viewing my father when he needed a wife or a mother. I was allowed a great deal of responsibility and privileges that my friends didn't have. I could buy anything because I was my daddy's little girl and his favorite. I was even in charge of the budget. As long as my chores were done at home, (dinner, dishes, housecleaning, taking care of my siblings, homework) I could go out and I had no curfew. I always enjoyed the fact that we weren't father/daughter, but that we had a very business-like relationship.

I remember being terrified of him, yet knowing that he desperately needed me. It was very confusing. I always thought that I'd stay at home with him and take care of him until I could find him a wife. I was glad when he remarried because it freed me up from taking care of household things. But then, he played her and me against one another because he liked it when we fought and I ran to him for comfort. I would like to heal myself from what my father did to me. I don't want to drag all of his shit with me for the rest of my life. "I am on disability and I can never have children due to all the damage you have done to my body. I have no respect for you at all. Though I love you for all the good things you did, you will never know that love because there is no relationship between us."

Vicky, 30 years old

My father is an alcoholic. Our relationship was horrible. He sexually abused me. It started when I was around four and stopped right away because I told my mom that my dad was hurting me. When I was eight it began again. This time it lasted a year. It ended when I went to live with my mom. Once I returned to my father, it started up again. By the time I was 11 years old, I went to the police. It dragged on in court, but he finally went to prison. One of my boyfriends was a verbally abusive drug-addict. Another boyfriend (the father of my son) didn't abuse me and listened to what I had to say. He truly cared about me. I wish I could tell my father how much he hurt me and that no matter what he does now, the pain will never go away.

Lana, 33 years old

My father was physically, mentally and sexually abusive towards me. I was scared to death of him. When I was ten years old, he told me that I was not his child, although I am. As a result, I have often felt unwanted in the family, especially by my father.

My parents were married for twenty-four years. Throughout their marriage, my father had several affairs. He is an alcoholic and was physically and mentally abusive. Two years ago, my mother past away from cancer. She was my life. I have not seen my father since I was fifteen years old. Unfortunately, I am also an alcoholic, though I am in recovery now.

My parents divorced when I was thirteen years old. Even after that, he would still come into our trailer in the middle of the night and physically abuse and torture my mother. He had homicidal tendencies and was more violent when my mom and

I did not live in his house. In fact, he almost killed my family and threatened to "take us out."

My most difficult relationship was with an alcoholic and drug abuser. He left me when I became pregnant, twice. The man I am involved with now is completely opposite to my father. He is a gentle, caring man and a good father to his two children. He is a protector. Over the past seven years, he has never physically, mentally or sexually abused me. He treats me with respect. I am not used to that from a man.

Thanks to my father, I am unable to trust men. I consider myself to be very fortunate to have the man that I have. However, I still believe that when I am around a group of men, my safety is in jeopardy.

When I think about my father, I feel anger, fear and hate. "You are the reason my mother is dead, you bastard. She was my only parent and I loved her. Fortunately, I have some people in my life who are my family. Because of you, I now have a dissociative disorder. I've had to pay a lot of money for counselling while living on disability. The next time I see you will be when I know that you are truly dead. You've ruined my life. Good bye."

Hailey, 21 years old

I've never met my real father. He left when I was eight months old. I will be referring to my stepfather, since he's been in my life since I was one year old. He is a convict-turned-preacher who brain-washed my mother into taking every word in the Bible literally. She believed she should could not question her husband's authority, even when he was beating and molesting her children. She believed she had to honor him, even though he was a hypocrite that led a life full of double standards and lies. My mother has always been afraid of him. He controls everything in her life. He treats her like a piece of trash. He's broken her down and taken her life away. She has no soul left. You can see that in her eyes.

Over time, their relationship has gotten worse. Although he's admitted to molesting me as a child, she's still with him. My

SHARI R. JONAS

mother is constantly wishing my brothers and I to die because she's lost her mind. One day, it just snapped. He still treats her the same way, only worse.

In my opinion, he is a lying piece of shit. He went to church and preached to everyone how they should live their lives while at home, he was sending his daughter into a life of suicidal tendencies. One night, when I was about seven, I awoke to find my father's penis in my hand. My little brother was asleep at the other end of the bed.

He was very mentally abusive, always telling me to work out because my chest was too flat or my butt was too big. In my freshman year, I wasn't allowed to leave my front yard nor was I allowed to play any sports because it would interfere with church.

He always looked at me in ways he shouldn't have. By the time I was fifteen, I couldn't take it anymore. I took a large overdose of pills and tried to commit suicide. Luckily, I didn't die, because it wouldn't have been worth it. Every time he'd settle down after beating the hell out of one of us, he'd always say that he did it because he loved us and wanted us to go to heaven.

My relationship with him was totally demented. I loved him, but every time he would leave the house, I would hope he'd die, I hated him for causing me so much pain and screwing up my head so badly. I had to kiss his ass constantly in order to feel loved. I just kept my mouth shut whenever my brothers were screaming at the top of their lungs, because he was beating them so badly. I hated him!

Once, when I was in sixth grade, he found my diary. I wrote that I had been kissing a boy. My dad beat me all over my body with a belt buckle, while my mother watched.

I'm very different from him. I'm against violence. I will never abuse my children in any way. I am kind-hearted and care more about the people around me, than myself. I love my brothers and try to help them. I am learning the true meaning of love and that is something we will never have in common.

Right now, my priorities are to keep getting therapy and become strong enough to press charges on him. The man I am involved with now is similar to my father. He is physically and emotionally abusive, controlling, angry, moody and has personality changes. The only difference is that he isn't a child molester. Other than that he is exactly like my father.

As a result of my relationship with my (step) father, I love men that beat me and treat me badly. I would rather be with someone mean, than nice, because that's normal to me.

When I think about my father, I feel hate, embarrassment, hurt, sympathy and nausea.

"I hate you. You have killed your children and your wife, mentally. You deserve to have your dick cut off and cauterized, an inch at a time. You are going to burn in hell, you sick f—k!!!!"

Tamara, 36 years old

I was sexually abused from the age of six, I think. I might have been younger. I'm not sure. It was by my father. He abused me a lot as a child. He would watch me in the bathroom and buy me sexy clothes and ask me to wear them. I would stay up every night and pray he would not come into my room. Many times, I would wake up in the morning and my underwear was cut in the middle. I cannot remember how it happened. One therapist said that I was repressing it. I thought that maybe my father was drugging me. I'm not sure, because I remember most of every-thing. Once I remember my father taking me to a place he called a hospital. But, it was not a hospital. There were men poking at me and all. It was awful. He even tried to hypnotize me. Many more things happened to me, but it's too painful.

When I was fifteen, I had heart surgery for a small hole in my heart. When I awoke from surgery, he was there abusing me. I had lost a lot of weight and he said that I looked good like that. It was awful. My heart is fine now, but emotionally I'm a mess.

I told my mother about this when I was fourteen, but she didn't do anything. She did tell her best friend who said that she was going to report him. So my mom made me write a letter saying that none of it happened. That was a hard time for me.

Just recently my car broke down and my dad offered to have it fixed. He said that if he fixed it, I would have to make him a dirty movie. I was very hurt. Lately, I've been feeling horrible, not going to work too much. I may lose my job if I keep this up and I can't afford to.

I don't hate my father for what he has done to my life. Most of the time I just feel bad. There's a deep emptiness inside. My father has been through a lot as child. I am thirty-six years old and I have a fifteen year old daughter. She is a good girl, but I do not feel that I have been the best mother in the world to her. I have a boyfriend who is very abusive to me, yet I still remain with him. I need to go on with my life and stop this cycle. What I need most right now is a good therapist.

Georgia, 42 years old

My father sexually abused me from my early childhood years into my teens and again after I graduated from high school. My life was one big mess because of this and I always felt ashamed and helpless. As a result of this kind of conditioning, I was continuously victimized by people. For many years I was confused about my identity and had no personal sense of myself. I followed every avenue looking for meaning to my life. I wound up with other people who had similar problems. For years I abused drugs and eventually married an ex-offender who was twenty years older than me. I was rapidly deteriorating psychologically because of never having treatment. After the death of my husband, I was left with a small child and was not capable of supporting myself because I was so dysfunctional. After using all the insurance money, I tried to work and support us but ended up in a co-dependent situation again, this time with an extremely abusive drug addict. The end result was that my child suffered a lot of physical abuse because of my drug addiction and my inability to tell what was happening, just like when it happened to me. Fortunately for me, I received a very large *sentence so I could get off the streets and away from drugs. For the first time in my life I was able to completely breakdown and cry, from the depths of my pain. I went through every program offered and extensive one-on-one and group therapy. I also began to develop my spiritual self to survive in my surroundings. I wanted to try to recover enough to be functional. It took many years and a lot of support and determination. Today I live on my own and I have my own identity. I support myself. I'm finishing my education and working toward my goal. I still have the bad days that every survivor has from time to time, but I know that the worst is behind me and that I never had to be the person that I was, ever again. Forgiving myself and learning to love myself have been so hard but so worth it. I want to encourage anyone who is in need of help to get it any way they can. So much of the pain that I experienced in my life could have been avoided if I would had gotten the treatment that I needed. Sharing my story has helped me. It's good to know that we are not alone and there is hope for the future, no matter how hard it seems.*

The Survey Says ... | 13

Having watched my fair share of the Academy Awards, I can safely say that the least interesting part of the show is when the President of the Association stands up and recites the rules and regulations. It might as well be dubbed over by the infamous voice of Charlie Brown's school teacher. You know the sound that I'm referring to the "wa wa wa" that comes from the invisible adult at the head of Charlie's classroom. I bring these points up as mere comparisons to this chapter of the book, where I explain in detail the results of the study. Although some of you might find it boring, I wouldn't be surprised if many of you find particular sections to be quite interesting. I've tried my best to keep it simple, yet significant. Glance through it. You'd be amazed at what you can discover.

Here are straightforward demographics about the women in my study.

Number of Respondents — **1015** : the average age — **29**

Marital Status
59%   Single
30%   Engaged or Married
10%   Separated or Divorced
1%   Widowed

Education
35%   High school
38%   College
27%   University or Post Graduate

Birth Order
48%   First born
13%   Middle child
28%   Last born
10%   Other

Number of Children
64%   0 children
25%   1 – 2 children
10%   3 – 5 children
1%   6 and over

Has Contact With Father
81%   Contact
19%   No contact

Frequency of Contact
50%   Daily contact
28%   Weekly contact
15%   Monthly contact
8%   Yearly contact

Presence in the Home (while growing up)
71%   Present
29%   Absent

Reason for Absence
76%   Divorce
4%   Death
20%   Other

Memories of Father
43%   Positive
12%   Negative
45%   Mixed

Of all the demographics that I collected, this last one, *Memories of Father*, has become the most significant to this study. At first, when I examined the group in its entirety, there wasn't anything particularly noteworthy. However, the instant that I divided the women up by their memories (of father), I found a wealth of information. Here's a perfect example of what I saw when I divided the women up into their memory groups:

Father's Presence in the Home (while growing up)	Present	Absent
"Positive memories of father" group:	84%	16%
"Mixed memories of father" group:	65%	35%
"Negative memories of father" group:	55%	45%

Reason for Absence	Divorced	Death	Other
"Positive memories of father" group	12%	4%	
"Mixed memories of father" group	25%	3%	7%
"Negative memories of father" group	32%	4%	9%

These numbers indicate that the positive-memory womens' fathers were the most present in the home and their parents were the least divorced. Conversely, the negative-memory womens' fathers were the least present in the home and their parents were the most divorced. For the remainder of the study, I kept these women divided into these three groups.

Marital Status of Each Group

	Positive Memories	Negative Memories	Mixed Memories
Married and Engaged	27%	36%	32%
Separated and Divorced	7%	15%	12%
Single	65%	48%	55%
Widowed	1%	1%	1%

Again, examining the subgroups provides us with more information than when we look at the group as a whole. The women with positive memories of their father are the most single, least married and least divorced. In fact, if we generalize this groups marital status results, we can say that:

- If your memories of your fathers are negative there is a 29% chance you will get divorced,
- If your memories are mixed, there is a 27% you will get divorced,
- If your memories are positive, your chances of divorce go down to 20%.

Now, that's an interesting observation!

Two Important Factors To Keep In Mind

The question, "Are your memories of your father positive, negative or mixed?" is more complex and subjective than any other in this survey. Unlike asking about education or number of children, each of us defines our memories differently and one word can't always summarize an entire childhood. However, it was an overall, general assessment of one's memories. I assumed that if a woman felt her memories were negative, they must have been. And if another woman considers her memories positive, then most of those memories must have been as well. Of course, when memories consisted of positive and negative experiences and feelings, then the appropriate selection would have been, mixed. The element of subjectivity is non-scientific, difficult to quantify and remains to be a challenge in the field of human behavior.

Another important factor to note is that this is not a completely random sample of women, as many psychology studies endeavor to do. Since every woman that responded did so voluntarily, knowing the type of study that it was and they all came from the same source (the Internet) this creates a non-random, non-diverse sample. This doesn't necessarily change the results, it is just something that should be mentioned.

Daughter's Describing Themselves

POSITIVE MEMORIES		NEGATIVE MEMORIES		MIXED MEMORIES	
Sense of humor	74%	Sense of humor	75%	Emotional	71%
Trustworthy	69%	Emotional	73%	Sense of humor	70%
Loving	69%	Loving	69%	Loving	66%
Affectionate	65%	Loyal	67%	Open minded	64%
Emotional	63%	Trustworthy	64%	Trustworthy	63%
Loyal	63%	Open minded	61%	Self critical	62%
Educated	63%	Affectionate	60%	Creative	61%
Open minded	61%	Generous	59%	Loyal	61%
Down to earth	61%	Self critical	58%	Down to earth	58%
Responsible	60%	Dreamer	58%	Educated	58%
Trusting	58%	Passionate	58%	Affectionate	57%
Creative	58%	Creative	57%	Independent	57%
Generous	57%	Playful	57%	Stubborn	56%
Respectful	56%	Down to earth	55%	Dreamer	54%
Easy going	55%	Responsible	55%	Responsible	53%
Passionate	54%	Stubborn	54%	Respectful	53%
Independent	54%	Intellectual	53%	Generous	53%
Dreamer	53%	Moody	53%	Easy going	51%
Family oriented	53%	Strong willed	53%	Moody	50%
Playful	52%	Educated	52%	Passionate	50%

SHARI R. JONAS

Strong willed	52%	Expressive	52%	Family oriented	49%
Devoted	51%	Opinionated	52%	Devoted	49%
Sociable	51%	Independent	51%	Sociable	49%
Stubborn	51%	Respectful	50%	Playful	49%
Feminine	48%	Low self esteem	49%	Trusting	48%
Intellectual	48%	Family oriented	48%	Opinionated	48%
Opinionated	48%	Nuturing	48%	Expressive	47%
Self critical	47%	Sociable	48%	Strong willed	47%
Competent	46%	Easy going	47%	Insecure	46%
Ambitious	46%	Insecure	47%	Feminine	46%
Expressive	46%	Anxious	47%	Low self esteem	45%
Confident	45%	Ambitious	46%	Artistic	45%
Sarcastic	44%	Gentle	46%	Intellectual	44%
Conversationalist	44%	Spontaneous	45%	Sarcastic	43%
Competitive	43%	Artistic	44%	Nuturing	42%
Energetic	42%	Feminine	42%	Analytical	41%
Cheery	42%	Flirtatious	42%	Competent	41%
Self confident	42%	Trusting	42%	Conversationalist	40%
Nurturing	41%	Competent	41%	Perfectionist	40%
Optimistic	41%	Devoted	41%	Spontaneous	39%
Gentle	40%	Sarcastic	41%	Gentle	39%
Artistic	39%	Conversationalist	38%	Anxious	38%
Spontaneous	38%	Analytical	37%	Ambitious	37%
Analytical	38%	Nervous	36%	Flirtatious	36%
Flirtatious	37%	Overwhelmed	36%	Street smart	34%
Moody	37%	Street smart	36%	Cheery	33%
Perfectionist	36%	Assertive	36%	Cigarette/pipe smoker	33%
Positive self esteem	36%	Outspoken	36%	Competitive	32%
Assertive	35%	Cigarette/pipe smoker	35%	Assertive	32%
Patient	34%	Perfectionist	35%	Optimistic	32%
Outspoken	33%	Short tempered	35%	Outspoken	32%
Street smart	31%	Self confident	32%	Confident	31%
Successful	29%	Confident	31%	Patient	31%
Religious	29%	Critical	31%	Nervous	30%
Good story teller	28%	Health conscious	31%	Critical	29%
Insecure	28%	Shy	31%	Energetic	29%
Critical	27%	Energetic	31%	Self confident	29%
Anxious	25%	Optimistic	31%	Short tempered	28%
Health conscious	25%	Overprotective	28%	Shy	28%
Shy	25%	Pessimistic	28%	Overwhelmed	28%
Driven	24%	Positive self esteem	27%	Health conscious	26%
Low self esteem	23%	Successful	27%	Cynical	25%
Short tempered	23%	Cheery	26%	Good story teller	24%
Motivator	21%	Good story teller	26%	Over eater	24%
Cigarette/pipe smoker	19%	Competitive	25%	Religious	22%
Nervous	19%	Negative	25%	Controlling	22%
Overwhelmed	19%	Self-pitiful	24%	Driven	21%
Old fashioned	18%	Controlling	23%	Overprotective	21%
Cynical	18%	Driven	23%	Motivator	21%
Overprotective	17%	Over eater	23%	Positive self esteem	21%
Controlling	16%	Patient	23%	Successful	18%
Financially secure	16%	Lazy	22%	Lazy	17%
Lazy	16%	Money motivated	21%	Pessimistic	17%
Money motivated	15%	Soft spoken	21%	Soft spoken	16%

Soft Spoken	15%	Cynical	20%	Authoritative	16%
Over eater	14%	Motivator	19%	Negative	14%
Authoritative	13%	Religious	19%	Old fashioned	14%
Dominating	13%	Financially secure	15%	Selfish	14%
Over achiever	13%	Over achiever	14%	Underachiever	14%
Boisterous	11%	Dominating	13%	Irresponsible	14%
Pessimistic	9%	Lethargic	13%	Money motivated	13%
Selfish	9%	Selfish	13%	Self pitiful	12%
Disciplinarian	9%	Irresponsible	11%	Addict	12%
Irresponsible	8%	Old fashioned	11%	Dominating	11%
Negative	7%	Addict	10%	Lethargic	11%
Workaholic	7%	Authoritative	10%	Disciplinarian	10%
Insulting	6%	Boisterous	10%	Over achiever	10%
Self pitiful	6%	Disciplinarian	10%	Financially secure	10%
Self righteous	6%	Insulting	10%	Cold	9%
Underachiever	6%	Underachiever	10%	Boisterous	8%
Lethargic	5%	Self righteous	8%	Self righteous	6%
Cold	5%	Cold	7%	Insulting	6%
Addict	4%	Mentally abusive	7%	Masculine	5%
Masculine	4%	Workaholic	4%	Workaholic	5%
Gambler	2%	Alcoholic	3%	Alcoholic	5%
Mentally abusive	1%	Masculine	3%	Gambler	4%
Alcoholic	1%	Gambler	2%	Mentally abusive	3%
Physically abusive	1%	Physically abusive	2%	Physically abusive	2%
Womanizer	0%	Womanizer	1%	Womanizer	0%

The Biggest Differences Between the 3 Groups

	Positives	Negatives	Mixed
Anxious	lowest	highest	middle
Overwhelmed	lowest	highest	middle
Short tempered	lowest	highest	middle
Negative	lowest	highest	middle
Nervous	lowest	middle	highest
Cigarette smoker	lowest	equal	equal
Self critical	lowest	equal	equal
Moody	lowest	equal	equal
Low self esteem	lowest	equal	equal
Insecure	lowest	equal	equal
Religious	highest	lowest	middle
Competitive	highest	lowest	middle
Trusting	highest	lowest	middle
Self confidence	highest	middle	lowest
Positive self esteem	highest	middle	lowest

This study found that women whose memories of their father were negative describe themselves as being more anxious, more overwhelmed, more short-tempered, more negative and less trusting, less religious than those who have positive or mixed memories.

SHARI R. JONAS

It also shows us that women whose memories of their fathers were mixed rated themselves as less self confident, having lower positive self esteem and more nervous than the other two groups.

Finally, we can see that the women with positive memories of their fathers rated themselves the lowest in all of the above negative characteristics and the highest in religious, self confidence and positive self esteem.

Daughters Describing Their Fathers

According to the women in this study, you will find that their memories of their fathers distinctly separate their father's personality types. A quick glance suggests that the women with positive memories describe their fathers positively, women with negative memories describe their fathers negatively and the mixed-memory women fall right in the middle.

POSITIVE MEMORIES		NEGATIVE MEMORIES		MIXED MEMORIES	
Sense of humor	68%	Short tempered	61%	Sense of humor	48%
Loving	64%	Negative	60%	Stubborn	47%
Family oriented	57%	Mentally abusive	58%	Short tempered	46%
Responsible	56%	Stubborn	53%	Opinionated	45%
Devoted	54%	Controlling	52%	Authoritative	44%
Loyal	54%	Insulting	52%	Moody	41%
Trustworthy	54%	Critical	50%	Controlling	39%
Generous	53%	Moody	48%	Critical	38%
Affectionate	52%	Dominating	45%	Strong willed	37%
Educated	51%	Opinionated	44%	Masculine	34%
Down to earth	47%	Physically abusive	44%	Disciplinarian	33%
Respectful	45%	Alcoholic	43%	Dominating	33%
Successful	44%	Cold	43%	Educated	33%
Gentle	44%	Selfish	43%	Old fashioned	33%
Easy going	44%	Irresponsible	42%	Cigarette/pipe smoker	32%
Financially secure	43%	Authoritative	42%	Financially secure	32%
Masculine	41%	Cigarette/pipe smoker	41%	Intellectual	31%
Competent	41%	Sarcastic	38%	Responsible	30%
Playful	40%	Disciplinarian	36%	Assertive	30%
Good story teller	40%	Insecure	34%	Successful	30%
Stubborn	39%	Addict	33%	Analytical	29%
Strong willed	39%	Low self esteem	33%	Mentally abusive	28%
Intellectual	38%	Womanizer	33%	Sarcastic	28%
Patient	38%	Cynical	31%	Perfectionist	26%
Old fashioned	37%	Self pitiful	30%	Sociable	25%
Ambitious	36%	Strong willed	26%	Competent	24%
Self confident	36%	Old fashioned	25%	Independent	24%
Sociable	36%	Outspoken	25%	Ambitious	24%
Trusting	36%	Competitive	24%	Overprotective	24%
Opinionated	36%	Masculine	24%	Loving	24%

Confident	33%	Pessimistic	24%	Money motivated	24%
Independent	33%	Sense of humor	24%	Affectionate	23%
Positive self esteem	33%	Lazy	23%	Insulting	23%
Analytical	32%	Money motivated	23%	Selfish	23%
Authoritative	32%	Under achiever	20%	Workaholic	23%
Overprotective	31%	Overprotective	19%	Negative	23%
Nuturing	30%	Assertive	18%	Good story teller	23%
Assertive	28%	Financially secure	18%	Cynical	22%
Religious	28%	Perfectionist	18%	Street smart	22%
Street smart	27%	Nervous	17%	Insecure	21%
Open minded	26%	Self righteous	17%	Alcoholic	21%
Energetic	26%	Analytical	15%	Outspoken	21%
Conversationalist	26%	Intellectual	15%	Driven	20%
Creative	23%	Anxious	14%	Family oriented	20%
Disciplinarian	22%	Educated	14%	Down to earth	19%
Optimistic	22%	Overwhelmed	14%	Competitive	19%
Cigarette/pipe smoker	22%	Sociable	14%	Trustworthy	19%
Short tempered	22%	Boisterous	14%	Conversationalist	19%
Cheery	22%	Self critical	14%	Confident	19%
Driven	22%	Workaholic	14%	Easy going	19%
Perfectionist	21%	Street smart	13%	Loyal	19%
Motivator	21%	Dreamer	12%	Playful	19%
Sarcastic	20%	Flirtatious	12%	Devoted	18%
Critical	19%	Independent	12%	Irresponsible	18%
Moody	18%	Conversationalist	11%	Cold	18%
Workaholic	17%	Successful	11%	Creative	18%
Emotional	16%	Competent	10%	Generous	18%
Health conscious	16%	Driven	10%	Religious	18%
Outspoken	15%	Religious	10%	Self righteous	18%
Spontaneous	15%	Ambitious	9%	Low self esteem	17%
Soft spoken	15%	Confident	9%	Dreamer	16%
Dreamer	15%	Emotional	9%	Emotional	16%
Money motivated	14%	Family oriented	8%	Self confident	16%
Competitive	14%	Lethargic	8%	Over eater	15%
Passionate	14%	Over eater	8%	Pessimistic	15%
Controlling	13%	Good story teller	7%	Self critical	15%
Expressive	13%	Health conscious	7%	Addict	15%
Artistic	13%	Overachiever	7%	Self pitiful	15%
Self critical	11%	Self confident	7%	Respectful	14%
Dominating	10%	Energetic	6%	Energetic	13%
Cynical	10%	Expressive	6%	Physically abusive	13%
Shy	10%	Gambler	6%	Health conscious	13%
Over eater	10%	Generous	6%	Lazy	13%
Over achiever	10%	Creative	5%	Womanizer	13%
Insecure	8%	Loyal	5%	Gentle	12%
Anxious	8%	Easy going	4%	Anxious	11%
Low self esteem	7%	Artistic	3%	Overwhelmed	11%
Flirtatious	6%	Devoted	3%	Open minded	11%
Boisterous	6%	Down to earth	3%	Artistic	10%
Overwhelmed	6%	Playful	3%	Nervous	10%
Pessimistic	6%	Responsible	3%	Flirtatious	10%
Self righteous	6%	Soft spoken	3%	Expressive	10%
Nervous	5%	Spontaneous	3%	Spontaneous	9%
Gambler	5%	Loving	3%	Motivator	9%

SHARI R. JONAS

Lazy	5%	Patient	3%	Trusting	9%
Alcoholic	5%	Positive self esteem	3%	Underachiever	8%
Negative	4%	Shy	3%	Patient	8%
Insulting	4%	Trustworthy	3%	Shy	8%
Selfish	4%	Affectionate	2%	Positive self esteem	7%
Mentally abusive	4%	Gentle	2%	Soft Spoken	7%
Irresponsible	4%	Motivator	2%	Over achiever	7%
Womanizer	3%	Optimistic	2%	Boisterous	7%
Addict	3%	Passionate	2%	Cheery	7%
Cold	3%	Cheery	1%	Gambler	6%
Underachiever	2%	Open minded	1%	Passionate	6%
Self pitiful	2%	Respectful	1%	Nuturing	5%
Feminine	1%	Feminine	0%	Lethargic	5%
Lethargic	1%	Nuturing	0%	Optimistic	4%
Physically abusive	0%	Trusting	0%	Feminine	1%

If we take a closer look at the most negative characteristics, here is what we find:

A Comparison of the Father's Most Negative Characteristics

Memories of Father:	Negative	Mixed	Positive
Short tempered	61%	46%	22%
Negative	60%	23%	4%
Mentally Abusive	58%	28%	4%
Controlling	52%	38%	13%
Insulting	52%	23%	4%
Critical	50%	38%	19%
Moody	48%	41%	18%
Dominating	45%	33%	10%
Physically Abusive	44%	13%	0%
Cold	43%	18%	3%
Alcoholic	43%	21%	5%
Selfish	43%	23%	4%
Irresponsible	42%	18%	4%
Insecure	34%	21%	8%
Low Self Esteem	33%	17%	7%

The numbers on these charts certainly speak for themselves. However, I believe it is worth mentioning that less than 3% of the "Negative" fathers were described as being affectionate, loving, patient, trustworthy men and less than 2% were rated as having a positive self-esteem. Conversely, less then 4% of the "Positive" fathers were described as insulting, negative, mentally abusive, selfish and cold. And, not one of these fathers was considered to be physically abusive.

Having read the data thus far, we can formulate several observations about a father's effect on his daughter's personality. A woman with positive-father memories acquires many of her father's positive characteristics and ultimately develops several positive life-enhancing qualities, such as self-confidence and self-esteem. A woman with negative-father memories appears to develop her own positive set of characteristics, which are hardly representative of her father's personalities and manages to have leave her father's unappealing characteristics by the wayside. However, possibly as a result of an unloving and difficult father-daughter relationship, this type of woman acquires or learns some negative attributes, such as insecurity and low self-esteem. As for the women whose memories of their father are mixed, they seem caught somewhere in the middle of the two groups. They have some of their fathers' characteristics, while they seem to leave others behind. Unfortunately, they do not remain unscathed by their mixed feelings and assorted experiences and they, too, develop several compromising attributes (anxiety and low self-confidence). It is imperative that we do not draw causal conclusions from these observations. Many other factors might be playing a role in the development of a woman's characteristics. We are simply making observations between women describing themselves and the same women describing their fathers.

Let's examine the types of men that these women became involved with. But first, I thought it would be interesting to ask the group what their *ideal mate* would be like. When I compared the group as a whole and then divided up, the results were the same. We all want the same type of man, simply, Mr. Wonderful. Here are the results of that question:

Women Describing Their Most Ideal Mate

Here's what women want:

75% and over	want a man who is: affectionate, loving, trustworthy, sense of humor, loyal, confident, passionate, responsible, playful, respectful, easy-going, patient, creative, generous, educated, devoted, gentle, open minded, down to earth, positive, self-esteem, trusting and self confident.
50 – 73%	want a man who is: family-oriented, sociable, expressive, successful, intellectual, energetic, conversationalist, financially secure, ambitious, cheery, spontaneous, nurturing, competent, independent, optimistic, masculine, artistic, assertive and a good story teller.

SHARI R. JONAS

32% - 49%	want a man who is a: dreamer, motivator, emotional, strong-willed, street smart, driven, health-conscious and religious.
14% - 29%	want a man who is: analytical, opinionated, outspoken, competitive, flirtatious, old-fashioned, sarcastic, soft-spoken and money motivated.
1 - 9%	want a man who is: overprotective, authoritative, perfectionist, cigarette smoker, overachiever, stubborn, shy, disciplinarian, cynical, self-critical, self-righteous, dominating, moody, addict, gambler, workaholic, pessimistic and controlling.
0%:	wants a man who is short, tempered, lazy, insecure, insulting, selfish, negative, alcoholic, womanizer, irresponsible, cold, underachiever, physically abusive, mentally-abusive and has low self-esteem.

It all seems pretty obvious doesn't it. But ask yourself if you've ever been with a man with any of the negative characteristics? Then ask yourself what types of memories you've had with your father.

Daughters Describing Their Significant Others

Before I begin sharing the results with you of the significant men in these women's lives, I must disclose what I decided to do with two-thirds of the adjectives in this study. Originally, I had chosen 99 adjectives for the women to select. There was no limit as to how many adjectives they could use to describe themselves, their fathers, their most recent mates, their most difficult mates and their most compatible mates. The complete list is at the back of this chapter. However, in the end I selected the 29 adjectives which were the most commonly used and most significant to this study. Half of them are clearly negative characteristics, while the others are distinctly positive. Here are those adjectives:

Negative Characteristics		Positive Characteristics	
mentally abusive	alcoholic	loving	affectionate
insulting	selfish	loyal	self confident
authoritative	critical	trusting	positive self esteem
dominating	insecure	trustworthy	easy going
short tempered	low self esteem	responsible	educated
negative	moody	respectful	generous
physically abusive	cold	family oriented	
controlling		devoted	

The Results of Chi Square Analysis

Christopher Benson, M.A. in Statistics from York University, Toronto, greatly assisted me in the analysis of this data. He strongly suggested that we use *chi square* analysis and I agreed.

According to Chris, this test is among the most widely used of all statistical procedures. In fact, it is based on a technique that was first introduced in 1900 by Karl Pearson, who has been called the founder of the science of statistics. The chi square test was one of the most appropriate tests — if not *the* most appropriate test — for analyzing this data because the data was categorical (it fit into mutually exclusive categories), it came from a large sample and lastly, the data could be cross-classified according to two criteria (such as self descriptions and descriptions of fathers).

The simplest definition of chi square analysis is that it is a test procedure, which compares observed frequencies to expected frequencies between pairs of variables. The expected frequencies are calculated from the observed frequencies using a certain formula. If the numerical value obtained from this test is significantly large, then the two variables are said to be related to one another (as is the case with the positive girls and their fathers). If the value is not significantly large, then the variables are said to be independent of one another or not related (as is the case with the negative girls and their fathers). For this study, I have used the word "similar" to describe two groups who were statistically related to one another. The following graphs show what the chi square analysis demonstrated.

Women with Negative Memories

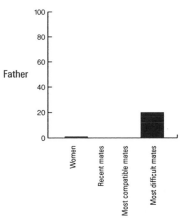

Women and mates compared to Fathers

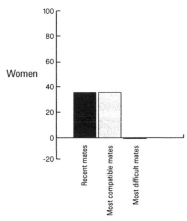

Women compared to Mates

The women to their fathers: **(1%)** Very few significant similarities (Exceptions: highly similar for: critical, moody and educated)

Their most recent mates to their fathers: No significant similarities (exception: moderately similar for critical, educated)

Their most compatible mates to their fathers: No significant similarities (exception: moderately similar: critical)

Their most difficult mates to their fathers: **20%** Similarities: physically abusive, insulting, negative, cold, unloving, not family oriented)

The women to their most recent mates: **37%** Significant similarities: low positive self esteem, insecure, loyal, trustworthy, respectful, family oriented, affectionate, trusting, easy going, educated, generous.

The women to their most compatible mates: **37%** Moderately similar: loving, loyal, responsible, respectful, devoted, affectionate, not physically abusive, moody.

The women to their most difficult mates: Very, few significant similarities **(-1%)** (Exceptions: low positive self esteem, educated)

Women with Mixed Memories

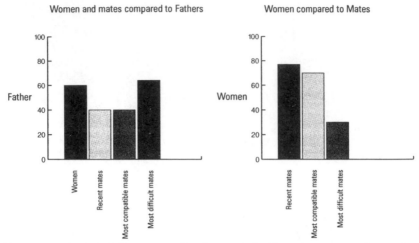

Women and mates compared to Fathers   Women compared to Mates

The women to their fathers: **60%** Significant similarities: short tempered, negative, alcoholic, selfish, insecure, moody, cold, loving, loyal, trustworthy, responsible, respectful, devoted, affectionate, self confident, easy going, generous, educated.

Their most recent mates to their fathers: **40%** Moderately Significant similarities: mentally abusive, short tempered, selfish, moody, trustworthy, loving, loyal, trusting, responsible, devoted, affectionate, generous.

Their most compatible mates to their fathers: 40% Moderately Significant similarities: moody, loving, loyal, trustworthy, responsible, trusting, respectful, affectionate, self confident, easy going, educated, generous.

Their most difficult mates to their fathers: **64%** Significant similarities: mentally abusive, insulting, negative, physically abusive, controlling, selfish, critical, moody, loving, loyal, trustworthy, responsible, respectful, family oriented, devoted, affectionate, educated, generous.

The women to their most recent mates: **77%** Significant similarities: insulting, dominating, short tempered, physically abusive, alcoholic, critical, low self esteem, moody, loving, loyal, trustworthy, responsible, trusting, respectful, family oriented, devoted, affectionate, self confident, positive self esteem, easy going, educated, generous.

The women to their most compatible mates: **70%** Significant similarities: mentally abusive, insulting, authoritative, physically abusive, alcoholic, critical, insecure, low self esteem, loving, loyal, trustworthy, responsible, trusting, family oriented, devoted, affectionate, self confident, positive self esteem, easy going, educated, generous.

The women to their most difficult mates: **30%** Moderately significant similarities: moody, loving, trusting, responsible, respectful, devoted, affectionate, easy going, educated

     S H A R I   R .   J O N A S

Women with Positive Memories

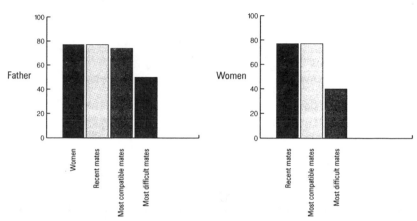

Women and mates compared to Fathers

Women compared to Mates

The women to their fathers: **77%** Significant similarities: authoritative, dominating, short tempered, negative, controlling, alcoholic, critical, moody, cold, loving, loyal, trustworthy, responsible, trusting, respectful, family oriented, devoted, affectionate, self confident, positive self esteem, easy going, educated, generous.

Their most recent mates to their fathers: **77%** Significant similarities: negative, selfish, critical, insecure, moody, loving, loyal, trustworthy, responsible, trusting, respectful, family oriented, devoted, affectionate, self confident, positive self esteem, easy going, educated, generous.

Their most compatible mates to their fathers: **74%** Significant similarities: authoritative, short tempered, negative, controlling, critical, insecure, moody, cold, loving, loyal, trustworthy, responsible, trusting, respectful, family oriented, devoted, affectionate, self confident, positive self esteem, easy going, educated, generous.

Their most difficult mates to their fathers: **50%** Significant similarities: mentally abusive, insulting, authoritative, dominating, negative, controlling, critical, loving, trusting, responsible, respectful, affectionate, easy going, educated, generous.

The women to their most recent mates: **77%** Significant similarities: insulting, authoritative, dominating, short tempered, physically abusive, controlling, alcoholic, selfish, critical, insecure, low self esteem, moody, cold, loving, loyal, trustworthy, responsible, trusting, respectful, family oriented, devoted, affectionate, self confident, positive self esteem, easy going, educated, generous.

The women to their most compatible mates: **77%** Significant similarities: insulting, authoritative, dominating, short tempered, physically abusive, alcoholic, critical, moody, cold, loving, loyal, trustworthy, responsible, trusting, respectful, family oriented, devoted, affectionate, self confident, positive self esteem, easy going, educated, generous.

The women to their most difficult mates: **40%** Moderately significant similarities: insulting, dominating, critical, loving, loyal, trusting, responsible, respectful, family oriented, affectionate, positive self esteem.

In Conclusion

This survey clearly illustrates how affected women are by their fathers. Women with positive memories adopt many of their fathers positive characteristics and consciously or subconsciously select men with very similar personality traits; similar to their fathers, as well as to themselves. Evidently, these same women are able to develop a strong sense of positive self-esteem and self-confidence. Is this a direct result of a father's positive influence?

Women with negative memories have taken a different path. Having experienced some of the worst personality types, they do not acquire their fathers negatives characteristics. Rather, these women consider themselves to be very different from their fathers. Unfortunately, feeling unloved or being abused by your own father does take its toll on one's self-confidence. Many of these women struggle with a diminished sense of self-esteem and are often burdened with insecurities and anxieties. Remarkably though, they are able to avoid getting involved with men who remind them of their fathers, as they probably would never want to experience a repeat performance of their childhood. Yet, not all remain unscathed.

Women with mixed memories appear to be the most complex of the three groups. They have aqcuired quite a combination of positive and negative personality traits which are strikingly similar to their fathers. Yet, they too, are plagued with low self-esteem and low self-confidence as a result of their turbulent father-daughter relationship. What is most interesting about this group is that they want mates who are "opposite" to their father's negative personality traits while maintaining his positive characteristics. Essentially, these women want to marry a new and improved version of Daddy. Many can attest that this is a difficult task. Eventually, mixed memory women select men who either have many of their father's personality traits, both positive and negative or end up with someone who is so opposite that the relationship ends in a divorce due to many incompatibilities.

Whether your memories are mixed or negative, managing the disappointment that is created by a less-then-perfect father-daughter relationship is quite a challenge. We hold onto those feelings because we want to heal. For some women, to heal is to seek out a man who reminds her of her father and hopefully fulfill some of her unmet needs. In other cases, women will go to the opposite extreme, looking for someone who is so different from her father, to avoid being hurt again.

True, a man who is very different from your father might not give you the same grief your father did, but how well suited is he for you?

What it all boils down to is that we should keep our father's personalities out of our mate selection process. Our focus should always be on our own unique characteristics and personal attributes. Concentrate more on your relationship "wants", rather then your unmet deep-seated needs. And above all, leave the relationship with your father out of the equation.

Now, that, is a real challenge.

Low self-esteem;
It's like driving through life with your handbrake on.
— Maxwell Maltz

14 | Living and Loving After Daddy

I am not afraid of storms,
for I am learning how to sail my ship.
— Louisa May Alcott

The greatest responsibility of all time is being a parent. If you have yet to become one, then you have only a vague idea. You might have close relatives with children or good friends who have taken the plunge into parenthood, but unless you become a parent, you will never truly understand the depth and magnitude of that duty. However, being that you are somebody's child, you know how absolutely dependent you were on one or both of your parents.

As I walk around with my baby girl in my arms, I realize that the very the existence of her life depends on me. Not only do I provide her with the sustenance that enables her body to grow, I nourish her with love, warmth and security, within a positive environment. I am responsible for her total emotional and physical well-being. This is not to say that if anything ever happened to me, she wouldn't be taken care of by her father, grandparents, siblings, etc. I am just amplifying the importance of being a parent. What a world we would live in if all parents believed this strongly in their responsibility. But, we know that many unwittingly have children without fully understanding the monumental task at hand. Ignorance, lack of education, selfishness and insensitivity can lead a parent to making wrongful decisions, emotionally scarring their offspring.

SHARI R. JONAS

Parenting is truly one of life's greatest challenges. To encourage the healthy, emotional and physical development of another person's life is both a short-term sacrifice and a lifelong reward. To neglect or destroy that process is a spiritual crime, punishable not by the victim, but by a force beyond our comprehension. Trust this process. You need not suffer for the thoughtlessness of your parent's actions by burdening yourself with sadness or anger. For the parent who empowers their child by cultivating his or her self-esteem and self-worth has surpassed all human endeavors. While the parent who attempts to annihilate their child's spirit, and all the beauty within it, must live with this failure for the rest of their life. You'd be surprised how the weight of that spiritual disaster can wear away at the heart and conscious of any human.

As I see it, spilled milk is an allegory for bad parenting. It has happened and we cannot change the past. What we can do is make a choice; to either clean up and move on or sit in our pool of rancidness. Some messes are easier to mop up than others, the magnitude of which has been presented in this book. Everyone and their experience is unique. Some women are more resilient and like Bounty — are quicker, picker uppers. While others take years to overcome the aftermath of a difficult, neglected or non-existent relationship with their father. Either way, the responsibility of resolving these issues rests on the woman's shoulders. But, it's not as difficult as it may seem. Investigating relationships and exploring feelings is not completely foreign to a woman. It is, in fact, quite common. What is unfamiliar is the individual. Thinking about your father, dwelling on what was, reflecting on what could have been and wondering why he was that way is not everyone's favorite pastime. Considering the chaos of most peoples' lives — children, boyfriends, husbands, bosses, coworkers, friends, close family members — who even has the time to rehash memories of a man whose present role in your life is so insignificant? But if you struggle with any of the following issues: low self-esteem, insecurity, anxiousness, perfectionism, excessive need to control, difficulty trusting and/or are consistently attracted to the wrong type of man, I have some bad news for you; Your past is trailing you like a bad scent!

If, for example you are involved with someone who is just like your father in the hopes of resolving childhood needs or filling empty spaces, then you are embarking upon an impossible journey. Your partner cannot possibly show you the love, attention and approval that your father never did. Imagine two secure individuals coming together in a relationship, starting on level ground. Together, they move forward, assisting one another over hills and across rivers. If you are insecure when you begin a new relationship, then your partner's efforts are focused on digging you out of a pit, to get you to level ground. Relationships are difficult enough already without having to deal with each other's past. Yet, the aftermath of your relationship with your father has left you with such deep-seated wounds, they've become part of who you are. Leaving it up to your boyfriend or husband to raise your level of self-esteem or to deal with your need to control is unfair, unrealistic and destined for failure.

If you are involved with someone who is completely opposite, then you might have an advantage. The study shows that women who are with someone different from their father have essentially chosen men who are similar to their own personality. This might explain why they are more content. However, unless you have successfully and permanently elevated your self-confidence, reduced your insecurities and curtailed your controlling ways, then you too, are still fighting old issues.

The key to finding love and happiness within yourself is to neither deny the influence of your father nor attempt to resolve the pain that relationship has caused you through someone else. This can be quite difficult to overcome, as both behaviors are often deeply subconscious. Don't assume too quickly that neither applies to you. Keep an open mind.

Here is a three step approach, which I strongly urge you to consider.

First: Acknowledge the experience with your father.
Don't wallow in it, bitch about it or ignore it. Instead, take an allotted amount of time and become acquainted with the gamut of emotions that you felt during the most difficult part of your relationship with your father. Here's an exercise that should help you to reflect. Write down the answers to the following questions on the pages provided at the back of the book:

1. How did you feel when you were with your father?
2. How did you feel when you were without him?

3. In what ways would you have wished him to be different?

4. If he had been that way, how might you be different today?

Second: Reflect upon the relationships with the men in your life.
Before answering yes or no, take the time and contemplate these questions:

1. Do you consistently find yourself attracted to men who are like your father or men that are vastly different?

2. Has any boyfriend ever made you feel the way your father did?

3. Have you ever treated a boyfriend the way your father treated you?

4. Do you find yourself needing a lot of attention, affection and positive feedback and that without it, you feel the relationship is not flourishing?

5. How often would you say that you've been disillusioned and disappointed by the men in your life — not including your father?

Third: Commit to change.
This is the hardest part. But, I have a few suggestions that might help you. One of the easiest ways to get yourself to change is to consistently talk yourself through it. Sustain a positive, inner dialogue. At times, you will feel empowered by your own words and plans. Other times, you will hear a weak and fearful voice, whose sole purpose is to doubt your every thought and action. Keep in mind that for every negative thought, there is an equally powerful positive thought deep within you.

According to the ancient Chinese philosophy of Yin and Yang, the entire universe consists of such opposing and complementary forces. We cannot experience one duality without the other. Lightness, darkness, coldness, heat, masculine, feminine, rain and sunshine are just a few examples. It is also believed that these mutually dependent opposites are represented within every human emotion, character and behavior. The following is a list of several yin and yang emotional traits and behavioral activities.

Yin	Yang
feminine	masculine
passive	active
insecure	frustrated
depressed	angry
tearful	irritable
sensitive	competitive
gentle	ambitious
imaginative	detailed
flexible mind	precise
creative	logical
weak	strong
chatting, reading	financial accounts
listening to music	computer

From the moment we are born, we either have more yin or more yang qualities, although we are never entirely without one opposing trait. To achieve harmony within ourselves, our yin and yang must be equally balanced. Too much of either is not healthy. You can achieve balance in a number of ways. Eating certain foods, redecorating or re-arranging your home or changing your behavior can all bring out the much-needed element in your life.

A quick glance at this short list can offer you insight as to which side your personality predominates and which element you are lacking. I have brought this to your attention because you can change yourself by working to balance your yin and yang. One way in which to begin this process would be to initiate the self-dialogue concept that I just mentioned, using your less perceptible inner voice. For example, if you are too yin, then your inner dialogue should take on a more logical, enthusiastic and confident tone. Next, your day-to-day affairs should incorporate more order, detail and goal setting tasks. Lastly, there are many foods, exercises and activities that can assist you in this restorative and harmonizing process.

Remember, you are not to completely eliminate any one of your characteristics, only minimize it if it is in excess and then adopt it's polar opposite trait. If your father has been absent throughout a large part of your life, it would not be unusual for you to have an excess of yang. Rather than living with a void in your heart, you have over-compensated with masculine traits. As a result, your feminine side is out of whack. It is possible to develop your yin side without feeling inadequate or vulnerable (although you might have trouble believing this). There are many wonderful yin activities, foods and characteristics that would enhance your feminine side and harmonize your personality.

Living and loving after Daddy is possible when you follow the exercises in this chapter.

- Don't be afraid to rehash old feelings about your father.
- Don't dismiss any patterns that might exist with the men in your life.
- Don't kid yourself about the effectiveness of positive self-talk.
- Don't worry about releasing excessive personality traits that you feel define who you are.
- Don't hesitate to incorporate new emotions or behaviors, which seemingly oppose your personality. Too much of any one characteristic leads to an inefficiency elsewhere. Being balanced in this way will not only result in greater happiness, you will become a magnet to individuals whose yin and yang are also in harmony. Honestly, what more can you ask for?

15

Doing
What It Takes

What would you think if I sang out of tune,
Would you stand up and walk out on me?
Lend me your ears and I'll sing you a song
And I'll try not to sing out of key.
Oh, I get by with a little help from my friends
I'm gonna try with a little help from my friends

— Joe Cocker

There comes a time in everyone's life when we admit to ourselves that we need a little help. Some people have a hard time asking for it, while others seem to ask a little too often. The human element that differentiates those who can from those who cannot is humility. Without it, your vanity, arrogance and condescension can prohibit you from becoming a better person. Although, you would be the last person to agree. However, those who are humble and modest can readily accept the lessons that the world has to offer, of which there is no shortage. There is a wealth of literature in the library, bookstore and Internet that offers guidance on every topic known to mankind. If you are a better listener than you are a reader, you can find a therapist with a specialty in any field of psychology, purchase an audio cassette with helpful advice or better still, have a heart-to-heart talk with someone older and wiser than yourself.

Some months ago, my wonderful cousin Rose had dropped in to say hello. Without fail, we got into one of our intense discussions in which we exchanged remarkably similar views on life, despite our thirty year age difference. Rose had had her fair share of life's ups and downs and I admire how she has managed through it all. That day, she decided to read to me a letter she had written to her granddaughter for her sixteenth birthday. I thought it was so beautiful, that I asked her permission to reprint it. Her words speak volumes as she offers advice that only years of experience can bring.

Dearest Jaime,

Having lived to the age of sixty-five, we learn all about life and its secrets. And there are secrets. The beauty in aging is we gain a certain amount of wisdom, not to say we have all the answers, because life is all about lessons and learning and no one has the answers. So, we continue to grow and learn.

It is most important to have good self esteem, believe in yourself and take pride in who you are. And self respect, if you don't respect yourself then no one will give you respect. And it is important to respect others.

People will come into your life through the years, some you will admire and others you won't — those are the people to avoid. Choose your role models carefully — those who are kind, considerate and who accomplish in life.

Cultivate your mind; it is your most powerful commodity.

Channel your energies into positive directions. We are on this earth for a purpose, it is not a dress rehearsal. We cannot take anything or anyone for granted. It is in our hands to choose the right path.

It is of utmost importance to have goals in your life and strive to achieve them. Remember that no one can make you happy but yourself. We are responsible for our actions and actions speak louder then words. I hope you will follow your goals and your dreams. Remember always that you are an intelligent and determined young lady and don't ever lose sight of that.

I hope and pray that you will strive to be the best that you can be and in so doing you will continue to be a great source of pride and joy to your family and friends.

You are a beautiful young lady, but beauty is not only exterior. It is within and that is what makes you a whole woman.

Best wishes on your Sixteenth Birthday.

If you want to learn about life, listen to those who have lived it, pay attention to those who have been through what you're going through and always keep an open mind. Most importantly, remember that the wisdom you receive is only useful if you apply it.

Which brings us to the next phase of this book. I have written seven *Mind Aerobic Exercises* that you can practice as little or as often as you want. Having read many books, I know that we don't always benefit from another person's suggestions or techniques. What works for some, doesn't necessarily work for everyone. But, if you find just one technique that modifies your behavior to some degree, then you are further ahead than before. And I have accomplished my task.

Practice Random Acts of Self Love

16

The way to be most helpful to others, is for me to do the
thing that right now would be most helpful to me.
— Hugh Prather

Often times, I experience something in its entirety, yet walk away only remembering a small fraction. For example, I'll go to a party and the very next day, there are only a handful of small events that remain in my memory. The same effect will occur when I sit through a seminar or even an entire course. Only a select amount of significant information stays with me. I believe the whole purpose of experiencing something is for those small details that you walk away with.

Relationships, of all kind, are the same. You can spend months and years with someone. But, when it is over and done, there are only a handful of positive memories and a handful of negative ones. For some people, it is the negative memories that linger. But, to those of you who walk away remembering the positive highlights, I commend you. For that, is what it's all about.

Here's an example; Imagine that you are packing a valise full of memories to take to a deserted island. Would you stuff it with the crap that you had to deal with from the people in your life or fill it with the fun that you've shared with those that you've loved? The relationships are the same, only the perspective changes. We *can* be selective about our memories. They are the backbone of our experiences and our experiences define who we are.

Recently, I read, *The Four Agreements*, by Don Miguel Ruiz. One of the most profound and memorable bits that I retained from it I have selected to share with you. Here is that excerpt:

"In your whole life nobody has ever abused you more than you have abused yourself. And the limit of your self-abuse is exactly the limit that you will tolerate from someone else. If someone abuses you a little more than you abuse yourself, you will probably walk away from that person. But if someone abuses you a little less than you abuse yourself, you will probably stay in that relationship and tolerate it endlessly."

"If you abuse yourself very badly, you can even tolerate someone who beats you up, humiliates you and treats you like dirt because in your belief system you say, "I deserve it. This person is doing me a favor by being with me. I'm not worthy of love and respect. I'm not good enough." We have this need to be accepted and to be loved by others, but we cannot love and accept ourselves. The more self-love we have, the less we will experience self-abuse."

Isn't that wonderful? Can you see why that one paragraph would stay in my mind? The limit of your self-abuse is exactly the limit that you will tolerate from someone else. Essentially, this statement is putting you in the driver's seat. The reason why you are in an abusive relationship is because you are allowing yourself to be there. The reason you are tolerating it is because you treat yourself or see yourself the same way as that individual does. How did you get that way to begin with? For that, we must look at our childhood.

Our upbringing teaches us how to love ourselves or to abuse ourselves. We learn this by the love or abuse we receive from those we trust the most. We learn this from our parents. But, what if our parents aren't capable of teaching us how to love ourselves? What if they have never been taught? Do we struggle through life without it?

When I was at the age to begin my driving lessons, my mother was still hopping in and out of taxis. If I had to depend on my mother to teach me the basics of driver's education, then I too would be hopping in and out of taxis today.

Our parents simply cannot teach us what they do not know. Just because they arrived before us does not mean they've figured it all out (despite what they might have told you). We argue and rebel when our parents try to teach us something and yet, blame them when they have failed to do it.

As a parent, I can safely say that there is nothing in the world more difficult than raising a child. We are bound to make mistakes. We can only hope that when our children grow up, they will realize that we are not perfect and love us just the same.

For all the important life issues that your parents might not have been able to discuss with you, there are people, schools and a plethora of resources ready and willing to show you the way when you are ready. Learning how to love yourself is an integral part of human development. Without this ability, you cannot have a healthy self-esteem and you will question yourself and your capacity every step of the way. If you can honestly say that you don't love yourself, then you must take the time to do so. It will change your relationships and your life immensely.

As Susan Salzberg so eloquently phrased it in her article entitled, "Opening the Heart", "We begin with ourselves because truly caring for ourselves is the foundation for being able to care for others." If you have difficulty with this concept because deep down inside you feel that loving yourself is an act of selfishness, you are not alone. Millions of women throughout the world have sacrificed their happiness for others. But know this; loving yourself is as vital to your personal growth as nutrients are to a plant. Yes, a plant can survive on water, but it will absolutely thrive with nutrients. So will you, when you can learn to love yourself.

Even as new parents, the first thing we are taught before we leave the hospital is to make sure we take the time to rest. The more rest we have, the better parents we are. For a rested mother is a patient mother and patience is what all good mothers have.

So, how does one begin to love oneself if one has never been taught? It's easier than you think. If you can first recognize how critical it is for you to take the time to make yourself happy, then that is half the challenge. The next part is easy.

List ten activities that make you feel good. Begin with the phrase, "I love to . . ."

Go wild with this, even if it seems a little unrealistic. Why? It has to do with putting the thought out into the universe. You just never know when a special random act of self-love will present itself to you. But, do list several simpler self-indulgent statements. The ones that take time out of your day, rather than money out of your pocket.

Next, I would like you to pick and perform at least one of your self-loving acts each week. As time passes, you should build up your list and the frequency of usage to at least once a day. It will take time, but be consistent each week. After a while, you won't need your list anymore. The things you love to do for yourself and with yourself will be ingrained in your memory. Furthermore, the ease at which you engage in your self-loving acts will amaze you. Be patient and trust this process. You will benefit from it immensely.

For many women, just writing ten self-gratifying phrases is nearly impossible. They are the same women who have been sacrificing their happiness their whole life. They have been conditioned to think not about what it is they love to do for themselves, but rather what they can do to make everyone else's life happier. These selfless acts leave only the self *less*; less nurtured, less loved, less fulfilled. Whether you fit into this category or imagine yourself heading that way, begin today to rethink and recondition yourself. Remember the quote from the first chapter, "The more self love we have, the less we will experience self-abuse."

> *Loving yourself lowers your tolerance for others who might abuse or mistreat you.*
> *Loving yourself will command others to treat you the same way you treat yourself.*
> *Loving yourself will free your spirit.*

Do this and not only will your time with yourself be more enjoyable, but the spillover of your new found inner peace and happiness will be felt by all whose lives you touch, especially those who you love the most . . . besides your self.

SHARI R. JONAS

Practice Asking Daily for Divine Guidance

17

He who loses money, loses much
He who loses a friend, loses much more
But, He who loses faith, loses all.

— Eleanor Roosevelt

H ave you ever wondered why people ask for divine intervention only when they are desperate? Can you explain to me why the vast majority visit their church, synagogue or temple only on certain days of the year? Let's not pull any punches here; when was the last time you had a conversation with your divine guide?

When I was younger, there was a television series called, "I Dream Of Jeannie". It was about a man who found a bottle and once rubbed, he released the genie who was trapped inside. As a result, "Jeannie" was to grant him any wish he commanded. Ironically, she referred to him as "Master." Most of the time, she would misunderstand his wishes and inevitably get him into more trouble than he was in. That was why he called on her in the first place. He was in some kind of trouble and she was always there to rescue him, much the same way that our higher spirits are called upon when we are in a dilemma. Everyone does it. If you don't believe me, just take your atheist friend to the racetrack and watch him begin to pray as his horse nears the finish line in a close finish for first place.

However, let us not generalize. For instance, I am not one of those people who turn to God only when the chips are down. I speak to my spiritual guide regularly and frequently. Understand that my religious ideas are not cemented in some scripture. I am simply a spiritual person who believes in a higher spirit, an omnipotent force, a creator of all living things. Why? It is my feeling and experience. I look around at all the miracles and tragedies of life and I can't imagine who else is responsible. So often I have heard people say, "If there is a God, why does he let children suffer?" "What kind of God allows famine, disease and heinous crimes to occur everyday, all over the world?"

I have read so much and thought enough about these questions, to which I have not found any justifiable answers. It is what it is. If there are reasons, they are beyond our human comprehension. Our scientific minds cannot accept the rationale behind God and so, we call it faith.

According to Webster's Seventh New Collegiate Dictionary, faith is a firm belief in something for which there is no proof. There you have it. I cannot prove what I feel and what I feel is that there is a great force orchestrating our lives — but not completely beyond our control. This is why it is important to share your thoughts, hopes and dreams with a spiritual entity.

I believe that journaling is a form of spiritual communication. Although there is no written reply, your thoughts are being sent to your higher self and that part of you is non-physical. Many people prefer to speak in prayer, while others are more comfortable to simply whisper in their quietest moments. Whatever style you acquire is fine, as long as you have faith in your heart, as long as you believe in your divine guide.

Over the years, many of my prayers have been answered. I feel as if I have been watched over and taken care of time and time again. Though I have had my fair share of difficult times, I have always managed to land on my feet. My attitude has always been positive, just as my lines of spiritual communication have always been open. As a result, even in my loneliest moments I have never felt alone. That is why I feel so strongly about this exercise.

Whether you believe in God, Jesus, Allah, Buddha or your own personal angel, just practice asking. Ask for courage, for patience, for love. Don't be shy. Ask for health, for peace, for joy. Don't ask just once. Ask over and over again. And be sure to give thanks. Continuously expressing your sincere gratitude is paramount in the asking process.

Thank your higher spirit for every blessing in your life, from the morsel of food on your plate to the start of a brand new day. Make it a habit. You will be amazed at how your prayers can be answered. They won't be answered within minutes. But with persistence, with good intention, much of what you ask can be yours.

The funny thing about asking for what you want is that sometimes, the way you get it is in the least expected way. Yet other times, it seems you get the complete opposite — just to teach you a lesson. So, keep in mind these two important factors. The first is to be careful and be prepared; careful for what you ask and be prepared for life's lessons, because whether we ask for them or not we all get enough to last us our life time. Secondly, do not become discouraged, as difficult as that may be. Believe in your divine guide and don't be afraid to ask for what you want and need. You will receive some of what you've asked. More importantly, you will feel as though someone is always listening, when the whole world is not.

Anonymous
"Daddy, I want to be able to love you like a daughter should. But I feel so guilty. You have never done anything to earn my trust or deserve my love. You have repeatedly walked out on me and never stood up for me, even when I was fighting a custody battle over my daughter. You think that just because you have your life together now, that's supposed to make up for all the hurt you inflicted on me. All I can do is pray that someday, God will take away the confusion, questions and doubts and give me a peace of mind in regards to you. I wait for the day when you realize what you have done and call me and take responsibility and show just one ounce of remorse. If that doesn't happen I just pray that when you die, I will inherit money from you. I would donate it to a home for abused children. It would be the only time in your life you ever did anything good for a child."

Don't ever underestimate the power of prayer.
— Anyonomous

Angels in the Alley,

Author Unknown

Diane, a young University student was home for the summer. She had gone to visit some friends one evening and time passed quickly as each shared their various experiences of the past year. She ended up staying longer than planned and had to walk home alone. She wasn't afraid because it was a small town and she lived only a few blocks away.

As she walked along under the tall elm trees, Diane asked God to keep her safe from harm and danger. When she reached the alley, which was a short cut to her house, she decided to take it. However, halfway down the alley she noticed a man standing at the end as though he were waiting for her. She became uneasy and began to pray, asking for God's protection. Instantly, a comforting feeling of quietness and security wrapped around her she felt as though someone was walking with her. When she reached the end of the alley, she walked right past the man who looked at her but didn't move and arrived home safely.

The following day, she read in the newspaper that a young girl had been raped in the same alley, just twenty minutes after she had been there. Feeling overwhelmed by this tragedy and the fact that it could have been her, she began to weep. Thanking the Lord for her safety and to help this young woman, she decided to go to the police station. She felt she could recognize the man, so she told them her story. The police asked her if she would be willing to look at a lineup to see if she could identify him. She agreed and immediately pointed out the man she had seen in the alley the night before. When the man was told he had been identified, he immediately broke down and confessed.

The officer thanked Diane for her bravery and asked if there was anything they could do for her. She asked if they would ask the man one question. Diane was curious as to why he had not attacked her. When the policeman asked him, he answered, "Because she wasn't alone. She had two tall men walking on either side of her."

SHARI R. JONAS

Practice Shifting Paradigms

18

*Daddy, I understand that you didn't enjoy your childhood
and that it left you with deep emotional scars that changed
you forever. I believe that you are a good man and a good
person. I just wish you would have been a better father.*

— Anonymous

When I first heard the term "Paradigm Shift" I was unable to comprehend its meaning. Racking my brain, I sat in my first psychology class, General Psychology 101, an introduction to the study of human behavior. Had it not been for the example that went along with the definition, the light bulb in my mind might not have lit up as quickly as it did. Here is the explanation:

You're sitting on the subway, minding your own business, tired and stressed from the day. At one stop, a family enters and sits down in front of you. It is a father and his four children. As you continue reading your newspaper, you become increasingly aware of these children. Not one of them is sitting in a seat. Instead, they are jumping, twirling and running up and down the compartment of the subway. The father sits, staring out the window, oblivious to his children's unruly behavior. Your stress level is mounting at the sight of these little tyrants. Just then, the gentleman turns to face you and says apologetically, "I'm sorry if my children are annoying you, but we just came from the hospital. You see, their mother just passed away and I don't know how to tell them, it's still quite a shock to me." At the next stop, he stands up, collects his children and leaves.

That is a paradigm shift and this is its textbook definition: "A paradigm shift is a movement from one conceptualization to another, sometimes moving 180° from the previous position."

To experience a paradigm shift you would have to figuratively step into another person's shoes in order to see the same thing differently, from their opposing perspective. In the above example, you can see how you might have become annoyed and irritated with this family. At some point you might have begun to prejudge the father and his inability to control his children. The instant you were let into his world, given insight into his frame of mind, your heart must have plummeted. Suddenly, you could understand why the father and the children were behaving that way.

Very often, we experience paradigm shifts while watching a movie or reading a book. Our perception of the lead character changes as the story unfolds. Just when you think you have someone figured out, another perspective is introduced and your viewpoint suddenly changes. Suppose you could shift paradigms whenever you wanted, under any circumstances and in any relationship? There are tremendous benefits to this practice. To know another person's viewpoint is to gain insight into that person's world and their way of thinking. Once there, we can understand the motives for their actions. Shifting paradigms sheds light, opens doors and gives meaning to mystery. How often did a friend or family member come to you with their version of an argument? To establish peace, you reach out to the other party. The story is not as simple as the last round indicated. It's multi-faceted, multi-levelled and has history abound. Shifting paradigms is easiest when the problem is not your own. It's the difference between being a juror in a courtroom, where you objectively listen to all sides, and to being the plaintiff on the stand who advocates just one. The difficulty in shifting our own paradigms is that all too often when we believe in something we behave as though we're on trial; defensive, argumentative and self righteous. Fuelled by such emotion, how can we objectively and rationally listen to another person's point of view? If we let down our guard, open up our minds and our hearts, what might we discover? That there are explanations for most occurrences, that no act is beyond redemption, that no single human being, even our own father, is without fault.

We all know that parenting is not an exact science with a precise instruction manual. Many of us had fathers who did to us what was done to them, while others just didn't know any better. Their ignorance does not have to become our own. When you can see something through someone else's eyes, your world will open up. You will learn that there is more going on other than what has happened to you, because it happened to someone before you and before them, and so on.

Problematic behavior has roots that go deep within a family tree. Difficult personality traits are passed on from generation to generation, whether they are learned or inherited. Nonetheless, keep in mind that people who cause other people pain are suffering even more, especially when they are family members, because they are hurting the ones that love them most. Other than hardened criminals, most people don't go around hurting others intentionally. They are just doing whatever it is they want to do, whatever they know to do, regardless of the impact that their actions have on other people's lives. We know that it's not fair. But, that's not the issue. Shifting paradigms answers questions. Why did my father hurt me that way? Why didn't he show me the love that I needed? Why did he leave us or beat us or drink?

Remember this example from earlier of a young woman writing about her father. At first, she is remembering him when she was a young girl. As such, her memories are more emotionally charged. But, we see that as she matures, she begins to shift the paradigm.

"My father's main role in the family seemed to be that of "enforcer." He was very critical, very controlling and easily disappointed. At best, my relationship with my father was strained. I never felt as if I knew him or that he knew me. I was hungry for his approval. When that didn't seem forthcoming, I went to the other extreme and did things I knew he would not approve of. What I disliked most about my father was that he

was a bigot. Even now, when I watch reruns of "All in the Family", I see Archie Bunker and am transported back to my childhood.

My husband is completely opposite to my father. He is extremely affectionate. He comes from a very close-knit family, although they have a few skeletons of their own. Where my father seemed to be either hot or cold, my husband is always warm. Unlike my father, my husband is rarely moody and is not afraid to take responsibility for his own actions and words. As a result of how my father treated me, I found myself screaming [away] from any man that resembled my father."

Here is where we sense her shifting paradigms. She is no longer recalling childhood memories from a position of a hurt child. She is an adult who can shift her perspective to that of her father's.

"When I think about my father I feel many emotions. Guilt, because I feel bad saying negative things about someone I love. Regret, because I wish it could have been different. Anger, because I see my younger sister is still caught in the web of trying to please a man that she will never please. Love, because in spite of everything, he is my father and I love him. I think he loves me too, as much as he is capable of. And understanding, because although I am one of those who hate it when people try to blame their own failings on things that happen to them (like my father has done), I do understand some of the reasons he was the way he was. I think that maybe, he did the best he could with what he had to work with, the tools his own parents give him to use and all the knowledge that a seventeen-year-old child possesses about raising a family. If I could say anything to my father it would be to ask him if I ever made him proud and if I did, would he please tell me about it."

Within seconds of imagining her father's world before she was in it, she moved from an emotional place of hurt to an intellectual and compassionate place of reason and understanding. Seeing her father as a human being with a difficult history sets the paradigm shift in motion. Rather than feeling bad about how she was raised, she begins to empathize with her father's difficult upbringing. You can see how her mood shifts as her perception of her father changes. It's as if she is saying, "Although he wasn't such a wonderful father, I can see why he became that way." The responsibility of her father's poor parenting skills becomes distributed and shared, rather than solely his own. Maybe, if he had been raised differently, with different parents, or a different set of rules, he might have been a different father. The mind wanders as it plays out different scenarios. The anger subsides. Compassion and acceptance emerge.

Put into practice this notion of shifting paradigms. When you find yourself at odds with someone, step right into his or her shoes. Begin with co-workers, then friends, partners and family members. Emerge yourself into their lives and imagine their circumstances. Do not think about yourself or your feelings. Only what they must be going through, where they are coming from and how they might be suffering.

Eventually, you should try this with your own father. To do so, you must imagine what your father was like as a young child. What were his parents like? What were his siblings and grandparents like? Envision the types of relationships he had with these significant people. Think about his education, his recreation, his social status. Did your father experience any life-altering occurrences, such as death, divorce, depression? Imagine his life up until the time he became a young parent. You must try to see the world through his eyes. Even if your father never spoke that much about his childhood, take what you know and imagine living a day in his life. If you begin to feel sympathy for him, do not stop yourself. Feeling sympathy doesn't mean that you are agreeing with his behavior as an adult. It just means that you are developing compassion for another person who suffered in their lifetime. It just happens to be the man that fathered you.

To live your life without concern for other people is to live a self-centered and shallow existence. You were not born like this. You arrived with the ability to love and to be kind. Whatever happened to you that changed you is only temporary. It's the cloak that you wear to shield your scarred heart. Whoever wounded you must bear their burdens.

This is a generational pattern. It is a cycle that will perpetuate itself throughout your family and your children's family and so on. Do not hold on to the anger or the pain any longer. You will only pass it on to the people that you love. Because you are teaching them that people who hurt other people must never be forgiven.

You cannot feel compassion for one human if you cannot feel it for all. Do not exclude your father from the rest of mankind. For that is all he is, a simple man, no different than the rest. Have compassion for him as you would for a friend. Make peace with him in your heart. Your children will learn by your example, for they see the world through your eyes. And you should see the world through theirs.

Jennifer, 29 years old

"My father was the authoritarian type. He was both frightening and funny. We were to speak when spoken to and do as we were told, immediately. While my father was clearly the leader, my mother was both submissive and supportive. What I disliked most about him was his wrath and unpredictability. My most negative memory was of him beating up my brother, and then turning on me in front of my infant.

Over the years, I dated some men who were abusive, like my father. But, the minute I detected that trait, I dropped them immediately. My most difficult relationship so far is with my present husband. Actually, I can't think of any characteristics I have in common with my husband. He is an extrovert and I am an introvert. He thinks there is something wrong with me because I like to be alone. I like to retreat and lick my wounds, rather than discuss emotional issues with him. He's superficial. I'm introspective. He's a feeler. I'm a thinker. Technically, our relationship is over. It's been emotionally over for me for the last fourteen years. The essential basis for any relationship must be trust. He's done many things to destroy my trust in him. He lies and does things behind my back, which I have specifically asked him not to do. When I hurt, he hurts me more, instead of being supportive.

As a result of my relationship with my father, I married a man who was the exact opposite of him. My husband has no desire to be the leader, to make decisions or to discipline our children. I now see that I should have assessed the good qualities that my father had and looked for those in a mate.

I have gotten to know my father as an adult. He has changed so much over the years. He's more understanding, more patient and more lovable. He is a joy to converse with and spend time with. He's more empathic now than when I was growing up.

My dad and I are closer than we've ever been. We live next door to each other and I love to go and visit him and my mom. I love them both very much. I have forgiven my dad for all the abuse. I am finally 'daddy's little girl'."

19 | Practice the Art of Letting It Go

What drives my life today is the energy that I generate in
my present moments.

— Dr. Wayne Dyer

Whenever I have the luxury of spending quality time with myself, one of the first places I want to go to is the gigantic bookstore. Once there, I treat myself to a delicious cup of espresso coffee with two squirts of vanilla and a dribble of caramel on top. Like a kid in a candy store, I stroll up and down the aisles in absolute awe. For one, I am admiring every author who published a book. I don't have to imagine what it took to get their project completed, and now it is sitting pretty on display in one of the biggest bookstore chains in North America. Once I get past that stage, I painstakingly decide the section where I'm going to hang out. No matter where I begin, I always end up in the self-help psychology area. I must admit that I am quite familiar with many of the authors and their titles. I have been reading books of that nature since I was twelve years old. I hold my father totally responsible for introducing me to the world of introspection. I still have the first book he ever gave me. It was *Notes to Myself* by Hugh Prather; a classic read as far as I'm concerned. In fact, several of his aphorisms have stuck with me for so long that I chose one of them in this book.

On one particular journey to the bookstore, I had my four-month-old daughter with me. My time, therefore, was limited, for she was sleeping and at the instant she would awake, all hell would break lose and I'd be out of there in a jiffy. I had already began this chapter on "Practicing the Art of Letting It Go", when my eyes fell upon a bright, yellow book entitled, *The Little Book of Letting Go*. I picked it up for a closer look. Wouldn't you know? The author was none other, than Hugh Prather. Thirty years later and I'm still gravitating to his work, this time for a different reason. On the back cover, Prather wrote, "The key to happiness is learning to let go." It sounds so easy. Truth be known, letting go can be such a struggle, particularly if you've been holding on tight for so many years. In fact, it's enough of a personal challenge that an entire book was written to advise and encourage an individual through the process.

However, letting go and letting *it* go are not one and the same. Prather states, "There are only three things you need to let go of; judging, controlling and being right." Letting *it* go has more to do with releasing all the elements in your life — past and present that hurt or anger you. "It" is the operative word in this phrase. "It" can be many things for different people; the pain of your father's absence, the aggravation of your boss's demands, the self-righteousness of your sister-in-law. Allowing yourself to be continually aggravated, frustrated or disappointed by other people's actions gives them power — the power to push your buttons and determine your emotional state.

Years ago, a close friend of mine would take such advantage of me that I would end up with a painful ache in the pit of my stomach. This went on for so long, until I finally exploded. Thankfully our friendship was able to weather that storm. But, I had to learn how to handle stressful or painful situations more appropriately. I couldn't walk around with it bubbling inside of me. When I did figure it all out, I was liberated; I was no longer a prisoner of someone else's nonsense affecting my state of happiness. And that is exactly what it can be, nonsense. If someone is selfish, insulting, opinionated, inconsiderate — it's their nonsense, not yours. You simply have to practice letting it go, whenever it falls on your lap.

If you've ever had the experience of telling a friend about something that was bothering you and their only retort was, "Let it go," then you know this is no simple task. To hear that phrase can be as infuriating as the incident itself. It's as if we need to hang on. If we let it go, we are not standing up for what we believe and what we believe defines the essence of our character. To even conceptualize the idea of letting go, we feel the need to be heard. Heard and understood. Then, we need acknowledgments, explanations, apologies, free dinner and so forth. Here's the kicker; sometimes you get them and sometimes you don't. What then? We didn't choose for the person to behave in such a way, but we can certainly choose other factors. Such as our expectations, our reactions and their durations. Allow me to explain.

When I was a teenager, my father told me something that I have never forgot. We were speaking on the phone, when he asked me the usual up-to-date, fill-me-in questions. I had just broken up with my boyfriend and so I told him that I was really upset. This is how he replied: "That's okay! But, how long are you planning on staying that way?" I was confused. My father explained to me that it's okay to feel a negative emotion, such as sadness, anger, frustration, as long as you don't hold on to it. That was my first lesson in letting it go. Everything should have a time limit, otherwise you are banking it. The problem with banking a negative emotion, such as anger, is that it doesn't accrue interest. Banking terms aside, there is absolutely nothing to gain from holding onto anger, or any other negative emotion.

In the newspaper, USA Today, there was an article entitled, "Holding a grudge is hazardous to health." It mentioned several recent psychological studies where the evidence indicated that people inclined to forgive others enjoy better mental and physical health than those who hold on to their grudges (Psychologist Michael McCullough of the National Institute for Healthcare Research in Rockville, Maryland). In one particular study, holding onto feelings of resentment did more than just worsen an individual's mood. Holding a grudge was found to increase the participant's heart rate and blood pressure as well (Psychologist Charlotte van Oyen of Hope College in Holland, Michigan).

What is the reason for the grudge in the first place? How did we become so angry or so sad? The answer is at the root of many emotional reactions and there's not a single human being that is unaffected. *Expectations.* They are the unwritten laws that create massive disappointments in our hearts and utter confusion in our minds. Parents are *supposed* to love their children unconditionally. Marriages are *supposed* to be perfect and last forever. Bosses are *supposed* to acknowledge and appreciate their employee's hard work. Children are *supposed* to outlive their parents. There should be no famine, no poverty, no weapons, no drugs, no rape — *ever*. Is it any wonder that we are an emotionally outraged nation that can't let go of our issues? For as long as we have expectations, there will always be opportunity for disappointment. Every issue or feeling begins with a simple expectation. A failed expectation leads to an emotional reaction. That reaction can stay with us for a moment or last a lifetime, it all depends on whether we dismiss it, address it or ignore it. Let's take your father, for example. You expected him to be present, to be loving, to never hurt you. He failed to meet your criteria. You felt hurt and disappointed. What can you do about the situation that will change the way you feel? You can't change what has happened. But, you can change your expectations and as a result, you will change your reactions. If we can let go of (or tone down) our expectations, we can modify our emotional responses and minimize our disappointments.

Several years ago, I became interested in Buddhism. I read from the teachings of dozens of Buddha masters and though I am not a Buddhist, I do admire their basic philosophy. The entire teaching of Buddhism can be summed up in this way: "Nothing is worth holding onto. If you let go of everything, objects, concepts, teachers, self, senses, memories, life and death, all suffering will cease" (Living Dharma). Our suffering, therefore, is rooted in our inability to let things go. Did you ever watch the Star Trek series, when William Shatner was Captain James T. Kirk? If so, do you remember the "Kling-Ons", the aliens from another galaxy? Well, they aren't from another galaxy, they exist right here on earth! We are Kling-Ons, in the truest sense of the word. We cling on to everything that has ever happened to us in our lives. Our memories are packed with details of what people did, how they treated us or made us feel. We are victims of our own clinging! Imagine waking up every morning without a bad memory of the day before? Children are very much like that. They don't cling to their sadness or anger very long, unless the events that cause such emotions are repeated over and over. But, for the most part, children are quite forgiving, which is why we say that they can love unconditionally. I noticed with my son, the ease at which he could forgive me after I punished him. My daughter, at only five months of age, would cry her heart out when she wanted to be picked up. The moment that she was, she'd smile the biggest smile, cheeks still wet from crying. If we can model ourselves after anyone, it should be our children, who love us unconditionally and never seem to hold a grudge.

Maybe you are of the mindset, that by holding on to the anger you feel towards someone, you're punishing that person or you're teaching them a lesson on how to treat people better. If that's the case, read this excerpt from Dr. Phil McGraw's book, *Life Strategies*.

"Of all the emotions in the human repertoire, hate, anger and resentment are among the most powerful and self-destructive. You may think that you are justified to hate or harbor rage against someone who has hurt you deeply. You may believe that they deserve it and are made to suffer by your hatred of them. But to do so, to carry and feel that hatred is to pay an unbelievably high price, for the reality is that those feelings change who you are. They change your heart and mind. Hatred, anger and resentment eat away at the heart and soul of the person who carries them and they are absolutely incompatible with your sense of peace, joy and relaxation. People are not built to be happy and sad at the same time. You either contribute to, or contaminate, every relationship in your life. If you're dragging the chains of hatred, anger and resentment into your other relationships, then clearly, you are contaminating them. You are eroding the quality of your emotional and relational life. Your task is to undo those chains so that you do not take those emotions with you into other relationships."

Once you recognize just how detrimental it is to walk around with the weight of anger, sadness, disappointment on your shoulders, then you will know that the time has come for you to begin to practice letting it all go.

The Buddhists have a method that teaches you how to let things go. It is called "Mindfulness." It means being aware of your emotions without being ruled by them. You achieve this by detaching yourself from your thoughts and your feelings. You know they are there, but you are not judging or evaluating them. At the same time, you are neither rejecting nor clinging to them. This allows you to recognize your emotions without being consumed by them. It's operating as if you are your own well-trained therapist.

Imagine standing in line at the supermarket. The woman in front of you is talking on her cellphone. When the check out clerk has completed her job, she tells the woman what the amount owing is. Rather than getting off the phone to make her payment, the person continues to talk. Eventually, she begins the search for her wallet, located deep within her purse. Not for one moment does she stop talking. Suddenly, as if the person on the other end reminded her, the woman dashes off down an aisle in search of an item she apparently has forgotten. You're standing there, witnessing this entire event.

What are your thoughts and feelings as you watch this person's behavior? Are you breathing and sighing heavy enough for everyone to notice? Wouldn't you love to give her a piece of your mind? Not if you were to slip into a state of mindfulness. If you could become "mindful" and not cling to any thought or emotion that might be rearing its ugly head, you could walk away from that scene without an ounce of stress, aggravation or judgment. You would be free, as if nothing at all happened. Can you see yourself handling traffic in the same way? How about your child's temper tantrum? Imagine that you could learn to put yourself in a frame of mind so that whatever upsetting, aggravating or painful incident came your way it could be dealt with and then released. Wouldn't your life be peaceful? Is it even possible? It is, but you must be willing to learn some techniques and then practice them as often as need be.

Become Mindful — Mindfulness should be practiced first as a form of meditation, in a quiet place where you can close your eyes and relax. For anyone who has never practiced meditation, I should inform you that it is not just for monks and the hippies. Simply stated, meditation is a form of calming yourself and you've been doing it every night of your life (unless you are an insomniac). This is your state of mind before you fall asleep. All you have to do is immerse yourself in that calmness at some point during the day, where you will not be disturbed. When there is silence, listen to your breath as it enters your nose and exits your mouth. Do this for as long as you can. When you have a thought, and you will, imagine that it is tied to the rear of a plane and watch as it is slowly pulled away. Into your mind it comes, out of your mind it goes. The better you become at letting your thoughts float away, the easier it will become to do this when you are not in a meditative state.

Learn to Breath Deeply — This type of breathing does more than just bring in oxygen. It releases knots, tensions, anxieties that your body is feeling. Unless you try it in the midst of a very tense moment, you will never understand the impact of it. The hardest part is remembering.

Use your Imagination — Whenever someone is really upsetting me, I imagine that person to be in a dark place. I don't mean in a cave. I mean it in the metaphorical sense. I use my imagination to envision that individual as being unhappy, alone, frustrated, scared and just plain miserable. Then I don't feel bad for myself, but instead, I feel pity for them.

Write — For those who will pick up a pen and jot down how they are feeling, this can be quite cathartic. Releasing your anger on paper is an emotional output that has tremendous therapeutic advantages. Of course, whether or not you give that paper to your target person is irrelevant. Writing it out is, sometimes, all you need to let it go.

As you practice some of these techniques, I'm sure you will begin to modify, elaborate and discover some of your very own. Even if it takes a while, begin by being conscious of your personal need to release negative emotions that confront you. People will always test your spirit. That is human nature. But, nobody should have the ability to change who you are. Practice letting things go and in the end, you will remain true to yourself.

The following is the story of an adult survivor of childhood sexual abuse. I felt very privileged to have the author send it to me. Not only does her story belong within the pages of this book, but it's place is right here, at the end of this chapter. If she can let go, then I truly believe that anyone can.

Floating in the Darkness
(a child's nightmare)

screams in the night
thump thump
coming closer
monkey has been bad
time for a spanking
no please don't eat me
floating through the waves
hot breath upon me
trapped in the waves
drifting, floating
comfortably numb
thump thump
behind me
breathing heavily
coming to eat me
can hear her screams
floating in the darkness

For eight years I couldn't bring myself to remember. For eight years I pushed everything to the back of my head, locked the doors to those memories and hid the keys. I seemed to forget. Mom and Dad thought I forgot. Even I thought I forgot, until one spring everything came flooding back to me like a punch in the chest. I still couldn't remember everything, but since that spring and the subsequent four years following, I came to realize it was not going to go away. The keys would reveal themselves and it became time to face the unthinkable, the unspeakable.

My memories of my childhood are very disoriented. I don't remember exactly when my experiences of dissociation started, I only remember that these feelings of unreality started after my parents' relationship became stormy.

My father developed a drinking problem somewhere during the first three years of my life. By the time my sister Kathryn was born, the problem was my dad became completely violent. Daddy used to come home from work late, radio blasting. He and mom would scream at each other when I was supposed to be sleeping. I couldn't get out of bed for anything, not to get my favorite toy, not to get a drink of water, not even to go to the bathroom. Otherwise, he would rip that leather monster from his waist and raise welts on any exposed skin. Even if we weren't out of bed, the slightest noise would bring on the belt. Every night we had to be good for Daddy, but never were we good enough.

I love my dad. I love him as a child should love a father, even when he hurt me I loved him. It wasn't his fault he had to hurt me, somehow I believed I was the bad one, that I deserved to be punished.

I had the same nightmare every night. It was always about a monkey. It was these dreams that made me afraid of monkeys. How did I know it was a monkey? I never saw it, but I was aware of his presence behind me, his breath hot on my neck, breathing fast knowing this monkey was "coming to eat me." Something was wrong. Monkeys don't eat people; even at a young age I knew that.

I remember in these dreams feeling a sense of unreality. In fact, whenever I got hit with the belt, I was aware that the leather was cracking my skin, yet the sensation message got lost somewhere on its way to my brain. Not only was it like a numbness, or a sense of paralysis; but it was more like all my senses just disconnected themselves from my brain, with the exception of my sense of smell. My vision and sense of touch were the most severely impaired. This sense of disconnections carried through other incidents as well.

I remember one nightmare in particular so vividly as if I had just dreamed it last night. It was remembered in the form of a

SHARI R. JONAS

flashback. I don't know how old I was, it was before my sister (before age four). I was in the bathtub. But I was floating on something. My face was to the wall and the monkey was behind me. I knew because I could hear him breathing and I could smell alcohol. The best way to describe myself was completely disconnected, like I wasn't me. What really echoed in my mind during this flashback was a girl crying. Somehow I knew it was me, even though it sounded like it was coming from someone else. I was separated from myself like there were two of me. There was the "me" that something bad was happening to — but, that wasn't me. It was the shadow of myself. The real me couldn't feel the pain. The real me was somewhere else, on a fluffy white cloud.

By the time I was ten and a half years old, my parents got a divorce. After the divorce, I picked up where my dad left off. I hated my mother, I blamed her and I wanted to live with my father. I loved him and I hated her. I took out years of rage on her, my little sister and myself. To this day, I feel sick thinking about what I had done to them. The only feeling that I can describe when I think about this is utter hatred for myself for being so out of control. I verbally and physically abused them both — as if they hadn't had enough. I abused myself by tearing out my hair, scratching at my face, any type of physical pain to alleviate the emotional turmoil. I never felt pain when I hurt myself, just merely a detached calm. I subsequently attempted suicide.

During the summer of 1988, I was hospitalized on a psychiatric ward. Therapists and nurses indubitably saw the signs of abuse, the physical as well as sexual. I never believed them; I denied everything. I didn't understand anyway, not like I cared about what they thought because I felt they didn't care about me. If my own father hated me enough to hurt me then how could someone on the outside, completely unrelated, possibly care?

Dad went to AA meetings and remained sober for the next eight years. Throughout junior high and high school I went through fits of depression. I never understood my reasons for *being depressed, although I thought it was because I didn't know what happiness was. Feeling bad about myself was all I knew how to feel. The dreams of the monkey stopped after daddy moved out, I outgrew the fear. However, I have never been able to recall any dreams I've had since the divorce. I did manage to push the first ten years of my life out of my mind when I started seventh grade. From seventh grade through graduation, I formed a couple of close friendships and I never formed any intimate relationships until much later. Getting close to someone was next to impossible for me.*

Eight years from the time I was hospitalized in 1996, Dad became engaged to someone much younger than him. In the spring of 1996, my sister Kathryn found out Dad was drinking again. My body shut down and I couldn't remember how anything was supposed to work. Somehow I found myself in the attic of Dad's place sitting in the dark. The memories came one by one. The stench surrounded me. I couldn't breath. I saw the leather monster pounding my bare flesh, cracking the sin. My sister followed me asking me what was wrong. I thought she was too young to remember. She remembered.

The past four years have been somewhat of a blur. During those years, I finally started dating. However, as soon as I got close to someone, I had to break up with him. I didn't know exactly what I was afraid of until I realized that I would break up with someone before he had the chance to hurt me and leave me. In January of 1999, I finally had my first intimate relationship with a man, to who I am currently engaged.

It was last summer when I had my first flashbacks of the sexual abuse. At first they were not visual, I could only feel the terror of knowing the monkey was behind me. It was last summer that I realized that those weren't nightmares, but real. The state of consciousness I was in led me to believe that I was dreaming. It was last summer that I realized that men from my parents' generation called that part of their anatomy monkeys.

It was last November when I had the visual flashback. My boyfriend and I had just come back from a concert and it was the first time he had a beer in my presence, since whenever I smell beer on someone I freak out. It was later that night in bed when I smelled the beer. I saw what he did to me as if I were an outside looking in. I was very young. I remember I was wearing my yellow nightgown with Strawberry Shortcake on the front. I saw him get behind me and pull down my underwear. I didn't see what happened next. That part is still hidden away somewhere. Then I was back in my body waking up feeling wet in the back and that wasn't from me. (This is still what took place in the flashback).

As much as those flashbacks frighten me. I feel a sense of comfort in knowing and being able to integrate what has happened into how I define myself. I still cannot smell beer without having a physiological and emotional reaction. My heart races, I can't breathe, I feel dizzy, then I feel a pinch in my neck and I completely freeze up. But, this lasts only a few seconds until the smell goes away.

I consider myself mostly recovered from the traumas since it does not hinder my living an almost normal, healthy life. I haven't had a prolonged period of depression in a long time and I never again considered taking my own life. It is my opinion that the best way to recovery is to face it all head on, integrate it and redefine oneself — not to push it away in another consciousness. I tried that. Between the ages 10 to 18, I "forgot" about it. But the memories never go away, they just fade into the background. From the ages eighteen to twenty-two, I faced it. I talked with friends about it and it is now a part of who I am. Of course, I am stuck with the stigma of having a psychiatric "label" and yes, it is considered a mental disorder.

However, I do not consider having a mental disorder to be an entirely negative experience. I believe that I have found the proverbial silver lining in the storm of my childhood. What has happened to me has made me a much stronger person and an extremely sympathetic listener. My attitude towards life has changed. The past is the past; let go and move on. I have too much to look forward to.

To accuse others for one's own misfortunes is a sign of want of education

To accuse oneself shows that one's education has begun

To accuse neither oneself nor others shows one's education is complete

— Epictetus

SHARI R. JONAS

Practice
Giving What
You Want

20

I cannot give what I do not have,
But from my heart, I can give what I want
— Shari Jonas

When I was a young girl, my favorite past time was trading stationery. It was the rave amongst all the girls. Whenever we would get together, we would lug a shoebox filled with stationery and spend hours in our bedrooms trading what we believed to be our greatest commodities. We had set up standards for which pieces had the greatest significance and which had the lowest, although none of it had any monetary value. Our rules were volatile and emotionally-driven. A piece of stationery that was given to you by your best friend at summer camp had equal worth to a piece that was one of its kind. Pieces that were cute but worn were more valuable than ones that were impeccable but nothing special. And you never traded a piece unless you absolutely got equal value in return. Every girl with a box of stationery knew how to trade. It was a girl thing and we understood the rules, however arbitrary they were. Here's how a trade usually went. If you wanted something that I had, you first had to ask for it. You had to know how attached I was to that piece. If I showed a willingness to relinquish, you had to pull out your best stuff. Then, you needed me to want something that you had. The ball was back in your court. Would you be willing to part with one of your precious pieces of paper? The trade had to be fair or it would never pan out. Both parties would have to really want what the other one had. Furthermore, both parties had to be willing to give up something that they really liked, in order to get what they wanted. Very often there were heated debates. But, in the end there were only two options — make the trade or forfeit.

Trading stationery was great practice for adulthood. In many ways, it became a metaphor for all relationships. Quite simply stated: If you want something from someone else, you must also be willing to give it away in the future. With stationery, one good piece deserved another. If you couldn't give it up, then you wouldn't get it's equivalent back. In relationships, your good qualities must always be presented and in most instances, they will be reciprocated. The good qualities I am referring to are the positive attributes in your self that you contribute to any significant relationship. Whether it is trust, dependability, friendship, love, compassion, loyalty, honesty or any number of virtues that are important to you in a relationship, you must be willing to give them away. And what exactly is at stake here? It's not as though you have only a limited supply of these wonderful qualities. Yes, there are times when you give of yourself but you don't always get back. That's fine. And, don't ever stop, because if you do you are changing who you are. You can, however, choose not to spend as much time with that person. As with trading stationery, we always have choices.

I would like to illustrate this point by having you undertake a quick and easy exercise. (It's vital that you participate.) On a separate piece of paper (but not your favorite stationery) make a list of all the qualitative attributes you would like to receive from the meaningful people in your life. Leave large spaces between each word.

Beside those qualities, leaving as large a gap as possible in between the two columns, make another list. Write the names of your immediate family members (even if you don't talk to someone), your significant other, your children (if they are young adults) and a few close friends. Make sure that your two lists are as far apart as possible on the page. It will be easier to read the results.

Here's the first part of the exercise.

1. Draw an arrow connecting the qualities that you give to each person on your list.
2. Draw a heart around those people who receive your best qualities.
3. Draw a square around those people who do not receive your best qualities.
4. Draw a squiggly line connecting each person to the quality that they give to you.

Here's how it might look:

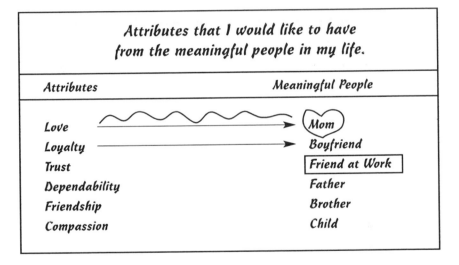

**Attributes that I would like to have
from the meaningful people in my life.**

Attributes	Meaningful People
Love	Mom
Loyalty	Boyfriend
Trust	Friend at Work
Dependability	Father
Friendship	Brother
Compassion	Child

It is clear to see that:
- I give my mother love and she gives it to me.
- I give my loyalty to my boyfriend, but he doesn't give his to me.
- I do not give my trust to my friend at work and she doesn't trust me.

Who in your life receives the very best from you?

Great relationships are those who you give your best attributes to and they reciprocate. Troubled relationships are those who you give to, but they don't. Eventually, those relationships will suffer because imbalance is too straining. The only way that relationship will continue is if the recipient offers you another set of attributes, such as financial assistance or another external variable. As long as the exchange has equal value to both parties your connection should remain.

The least functional relationships are those who you give very little or nothing at all. Take a closer look at those failing relationships. Do you notice that those individuals to whom you give very little, give you very little in return? That is why I refer to them as failing. If you continue to neglect each other, as you have been, then the relationship has no future but to fail.

Yes, I know. You are waiting for that person to come to you first and then you will gladly reciprocate. But, that is a dream. People have wasted years waiting for the other person to make the first move, only to wish they had done it themselves, as they lay breathless on their deathbed. Don't let this happen to you. If you want to rebuild or establish a relationship with someone, you must give what you want. Do not wait for him or her to reach out first. You begin the process. Remember, you have nothing to lose because you are giving from the bottomless pit of your good virtues. If you are a loving, compassionate and trustworthy person, you can never run out of your self. At worst, if you do not receive anything at all in return, then all you have is the knowledge that you gave it your best. A bruised ego is only an expression. In reality, no amount of rejection will ever change the essence of your character. Remember, it will always be the other person who has lost out.

In the practice of giving what you want, there are a handful of simple rules.

First: *Give in small doses.*
Never bombard anyone with love, attention, kindness, friendship etc. It seems unnatural to be so giving to someone with who you are attempting to reconnect. It will only make him uncomfortable. Over doing is over kill.

SHARI R. JONAS

Second: *Go slow with what you offer.*

Take your time. Mending relationships is very much like building a house. You dig, you lay foundation and you build the structure, brick by brick, never once forgetting to mortar each one in place. If you offer your friendship, begin by being a good listener. Don't run around doing errands and favors. People can easily take advantage of one's good virtues.

Third: *Be patient.*

You mustn't anticipate anything in return. Give what you want without any expectations. Expectations only lead to disappointment. You are reconnecting with someone with whom you have a history. Only time will tell where this new start will take you.

Several years ago, my father and I had stopped communicating. I was upset with how he handled a situation and we couldn't seem to get past it. We needed a cooling off period and it lasted over one year. If I had waited for my father to approach me, I might still be waiting. He's as stubborn and self-righteous as an old goat. Instead, I made the first move. Although my father and his wife live in another country, my stepmother's father lived in the same city as me. Glancing through the newspaper one day, I read that this gentleman had passed away and his funeral was to be held the next day. It felt so strange that my father was going to be in my neck of the woods and I wouldn't be seeing him. Of course, he wouldn't call me. But, in practicing what I believe, I decided that I was going to start the process of reconnecting with him by attending his father-in-law's funeral. It would be a small act of kindness, but certainly a significant one.

I sat in the back row and I watched my father. My heart was racing. Could he see me? If he did, would he talk to me? Though I felt sure about being there, I certainly felt awkward and alone. Deep down I knew that though my father might not stop to smile or say hello, in his heart he would be happy that I was there. But, was I kidding myself? Only time would tell. All I knew was that I was giving my father what I would have wanted, respect and courtesy. If someone important to me had passed away, I would hope that my father would attend — whether or not we were talking to one another. It is the right thing to do. I gave to my father what I would want in return.

My father never did acknowledge me at the funeral. Weeks later, I telephoned him to say hello. Our telephone conversations became regular and six months later, I flew down to spend my birthday with him. We managed to rebuild a stronger relationship than the one we had before.

If you practice this philosophy on someone with whom you have a failing relationship, you will soon discover the power in giving. We often think of giving in the material or financial sense. This is different. Here, we are giving of our personal self. In so doing, we teach people how to treat people. A large part of learning is in modelling. We set an example, a model of how people should give of themselves in a relationship. The best part is you don't have to think too hard about what it is you should teach each person. Just give what you want in return. If it's love, respect, honesty, friendship, intimacy, trust, loyalty, compassion, integrity, reliability or acceptance, give it. Teach it. And watch what happens.

Sharon, 44 years old

I now recognize that all men are not the same and life is what you make of it and not what you think you are owed. True happiness comes when you give of yourself. Do things for the right reasons, be true to yourself and recognize that you are whoever you decide to be. You don't have to be a bi-product of your parents. You can break the cycle, you can be free from the past and free to be everything you ever dreamed you could be.

Practice Wearing Your Heart On Your Sleeve

21

Every generation blames the one before
And all of their frustrations come beating on your door
I know that I'm prisoner to all my Father held so dear
I know that I'm hostage to all his hopes and fears
I just wish I could have told him
In the living years

— Michael Rutherford

I am a firm believer that children are amongst our greatest teachers. If you don't agree with me, spend some quality time with one. In so doing, you will discover that there are several aspects of a child's nature from which we can learn, from their curiosity and candidness to their innocence and openness. Of the many wonders that I've witnessed from having children, the one that has never ceased to amaze me is how they are able to display a range of emotions at the drop of a hat. They could be smiling and giggling one minute and then within seconds, big tears are rolling down their cherub cheeks. Whatever emotional state they're in, be it joyfulness, contentment, sadness, anger, frustration or disappointment, the message is generally clear. If a child is feeling it, the adult will know. Even children, born deaf and blind can demonstrate their emotions. Imagine, they have never seen a smile or heard the sound of laughter and yet, they exhibit both emotional responses.

For decades now, researchers have been studying emotions in humans, debating whether they were inherent or learned. Over time, the results became unanimous. We are all born with emotions. And the ability to express our emotions is innate and universal.

However, the context wherein we express our emotions are in fact learned. Our family, our culture and our gender are all factors that contribute to how and when we communicate. Some learn early, while others are late bloomers. Some need only a few lessons, while others can take repetitive emotional beatings. Some learn to disguise and conceal their true feelings, while others learn to shut down completely. But, eventually all of us learn to modify the expression of our emotions, self-taught by our own experiences.

How do we progress from being an open and emotional child to a reserved and selectively expressive adult? It all begins with an event that makes us feel insignificant. Youthful and resilient, we overcome it and like a puppy dog, we go running back for more. Then another incident occurs which makes us feel unloved. We're becoming apprehensive, but still forge ahead. Another experience transpires that damages our self-worth. The memory of that pain is etched in our minds. Our guard goes up. We commit to never letting anyone ever hurt us again. We become cautious as to whom we reveal our emotions. Only for a select few do we open up, if at all. We have lost trust in the whole world because of the pain caused by a small handful. We know we are generalizing. But, this is human nature. We've been hurt and we don't want to feel that way again. We must protect ourselves from the possibility of such circumstances ever repeating. Emotional withdrawal is a defense mechanism that holds the memory of painful experiences solely accountable. The heart that we once wore on our sleeve is now neatly tucked away.

At first glance, it can be difficult to assess whether someone is emotionally expressive, apprehensive or completely closed. A wise, elderly man once told me that he could read my forehead like a cash register. By the sound in his voice and not by the words in that sentence, I understood what he meant. I have the type of face that tells you how I'm generally feeling. When I am delighted, distressed or disgruntled there's no hiding it. Whether I am ready and willing to talk to anyone about what my face is revealing is another story. I too, have learned how to modify.

SHARI R. JONAS

On the other end of the spectrum, there are people who have what is commonly referred to as a "poker face." You couldn't tell whether they had a royal flush of a day or one that they'd rather fold. The problem with the poker-face people is that you never know what they want, need, like or dislike. You spend more time guessing and assuming than communicating and collaborating.

Do you ever notice how poker-face people are attracted to the cash register kind? Do you know why? We relieve them. We speak for them, socialize for them, get angry with others for them and generally make their life easier. But those of us who wear our hearts on our sleeve more often than not end up drained by those who conceal theirs. We're like emotional dentists, pulling feelings rather than teeth and getting paid in frustration rather than money. But, just imagine how they must feel? Unable to open up and share their intimate feelings, they are prisoners of their own past.

I have a friend whose parents are Holocaust survivors. They were robbed of everything that had meant anything to them: their parents, their dignity, their homes and much more. As a result, my friend was raised in a family where there was very little demonstration of emotion. Positive emotions were especially taboo. She spent the first twenty years of her life with minimal affection, infrequent smiles and rarely any sounds of laughter. Conversations were void of feeling, only courteous and factual. Needless to say, she has developed into a quiet and reserved adult. She never appears too happy, too sad or too distraught. Furthermore, all of her relationships are challenged by her inability to express her emotional disposition. She protects herself from anyone who attempts to get too close by keeping most of what she feels in closed quarters. Her parents have taught her well. Unfortunately, she suffers in her silenced emotional state, as do thousands of others who would rather remain impassive than wear their hearts on their sleeve.

But then, why bother being expressive? Today, more than ever, our children are growing up in a world filled with representation. There is a spokesperson for every community and organization in North America. If you agree on something or you don't, there is going to be someone ready and willing to speak out on your behalf. For years, women, gays and ethnic minorities were led to believe that their opinions didn't matter. We all had to fight for our right to speak. Now, we have a representative screaming on every rooftop. We're even sending our agents to other countries to assist them in their right to express their viewpoints. This is progress. However, there's just one minor setback. When the problem is within our own backyard, we shut down. For an environmental cause we become passionate, for personal disappointments created by one individual, we become impassive. Lets face it — it's easy to hide behind committees, organizations and support networks because there is strength in numbers. Rejection is manageable when it is shared. Confrontations are tolerable when the attack is via newsletter. But, to face someone who has hurt you and tell them how you feel is one of the greatest personal challenges you will ever tackle. If you are willing, then the only question you have to ask is, "How?"

Begin the practice of wearing your heart on your sleeve. As you feel, so shall you speak. Be true to your feelings, just as a child would. Be honest about who you are and how you feel. Don't walk around with your emotions tucked away in the recesses of your mind. If there is someone you love, then tell them. If another has hurt you, confront them. Any significant association you have with another person merits you being completely open with your feelings, positive or negative. What's the point in withholding? Lighten your load and let the person know how you feel.

To many, the idea of wearing their heart on their sleeve is frightening. It makes them feel vulnerable, exposed and at risk for being hurt — again. Imagine sharing your intimate feelings with someone and they don't feel the same way? How humiliating? Correction. How positive! Now, you don't have to waste any more of your precious time. Or would you rather keep pretending? The truth is only painful for a short while. Then, it is enlightening for the cloak of deception has been lifted. As the saying goes, the truth shall set you free.

But, what about their feelings? If expressing your emotions brings sadness to another, is it still so rewarding? There will always be topics which deserve discretion. If you are ever so uncertain, speak first to someone you admire. Their opinion might shed the necessary light. In every instance, you must always use tact. Speak to that individual with compassion. In the end, they will be as appreciative with your honesty as you are relieved about releasing it.

Consider now, the upside. Sharing personal feelings with someone who responds positively to you is incredibly rewarding. Progress is in motion. The wheels of communication are churning. You receive feedback and from there you can make decisions. Do you continue the relationship with a fresh new start or just maintain open lines of communication? In any case, it is a win-win situation for your frame of mind and well-being. You have succeeded at tackling one of your greatest personal challenges — you spoke your mind to someone who disappointed you. Once again, you have become your own representative. Only this time, you are grown up.

Here's your first challenge. *Write a letter to your father.* Some of you might have done this already, while many of you have only thought about it. Keep in mind that this exercise is very therapeutic. It might be difficult at first, but you will find it very liberating in the end. Most importantly, it will begin the process of getting emotional issues off your chest and out of your head. You will experience the sensation of gathering your thoughts and expressing your feelings. That is precisely what wearing your heart on your sleeve is all about.

Write your letter on the pages found at the end of this chapter. The reason I am suggesting this is because it is absolutely, unnecessary to send it to him. The completion of this letter is meant to provide you with a sense of relief, empowerment and possible closure. You, not your father.

Begin by writing how it felt to be his daughter. How did your father hurt you? At what age did these events transpire? Make sure that these are your memories and not what others have told you. What impact did your father's actions have on your personality, your relationships, your career and your life choices? You can be as angry as you want to be, **but you must also write something positive.** What did you discover about yourself? Which of your positive attributes developed because of your father? Maybe you learned what not to do or how not to be. There's no way that you haven't learned something incredibly beneficial. Write whatever comes to mind. Finish the letter and turn the page.

Your life is a book, with each experience representing another chapter. Some last longer than others, but every chapter must come to an end. Writing a letter to your father will assist you in closing this chapter. Before you begin, here is the letter that I wrote (but never sent) to my father.

Dear Daddy,

There never seems to be a good time to tell someone the truth. That is why most people never do. But I need to tell you how it felt to be your daughter. From the moment you left, I was a different child. I wondered where you were everyday and why you didn't stay. In your absence, I developed insecurities. I wasn't sure about myself. I always needed to have a boyfriend, a male companion in my life, to make me feel secure. I loved being in love and yet, I walked away from every relationship. I needed to be the one to leave. I couldn't bear the thought of being hurt again. As a young adult, I developed control issues. I wanted to be the master of my domain. Being in control meant no surprises. Growing up with you as a father provided me with an incredible sense of instability and uncertainty. So, I made sure that my children had neither of those qualities in their father. But growing up without you in my life, everyday, taught me a great deal. When a person loses their eyesight, their other senses become more acute. Without you around, I developed other strengths. I became a very resilient little girl. I learned how to bounce back when the chips were down. I became curious about the world, about people and their relationships. I learned how to communicate my feeling (I became a writer). I learned how to motivate myself, when no one else could. I came to know that I was different from my friends and that was okay. I developed an open mind and a compassionate heart. I became a great listener. I've chosen a career that helps other people overcome their struggles. Last, but not least, I truly understand how much children need their parent's consistent love, attention and presence in their life.

Over the years, as I've come to know you, as a person, I've discovered that we have a lot in common and that made me feel connected to you. But, I am no blind fool. I am aware of all your faults and still, I have accepted you. Daddy, the essence of who you are has taught me many things. You have shaped my character immensely. I am not a little girl anymore. I've grown up and in so doing, I have made my fair share of mistakes. I know that no one is perfect. Although I am a good parent, it is by far, the greatest challenge. Yet, nothing in life is easy. But, many things are worth it.

As an adult now, I enjoy our friendship. I am grateful to have such a special relationship with you. You are always there when I need you. You are a rock in my life and I truly love you. But more importantly, I thank you. For I am proud of who I am today. I am who I am, in part, because of the experience I had with you.

Your daughter,
Shari

Practice the Art of Being Perfect

22

I keep my ideals, because in spite of everything, I still believe that people are really good at heart.

— Anne Frank

This is the trickiest one of all. If you can perfect the art of being perfect, then it is imperative that you contact me. My email address is at the back of this book. You might as well notify the Guinness World Book of Records, because to date there isn't a single human being who has achieved perfection. Although, I'm sure many believe otherwise.

Just because no one has done this before doesn't mean you shouldn't try. For this exercise, it's quite essential that you do. Only then will you realize how impossible it is to be perfect. You might be excellent in your profession, superb in the kitchen or even phenomenal in the bedroom. But I would like to know if you are near perfect as a parent. And, if you are not as of yet, do you aspire to be?

I can safely say that parenting is one of the most difficult and selfless acts known to mankind. It is a full time, rain or shine, in sickness or in health responsibility. Just when you think you've figured out something or someone, along comes another challenge. It's a never-ending test of your patience, your love and your character. You only thought you knew yourself and then you became a parent. What a life-altering, personality-shifting experience. If you accomplish one-tenth of what you'd hope for in your role as parent, then I salute you.

Needless to say, there is a good and sincere reason for this exercise. As children we develop tremendous expectations of our parents. They are pillars of strength, with unlimited knowledge and exemplary social role-models. They can make anything better, from sad days and bad dreams to bruised knees and sore egos. We could never imagine our life without them in it.

Then suddenly, we discover a glitch in their profile. We are disappointed, but our unwavering love resurrects our illusions. As time passes, incremental revelations occur suggesting our parents are not flawless human beings. Each time, we find ourselves rationalizing in their defense.

Then we become adolescents and overnight, we find out that our parents cannot do anything right. We're enraged and disappointed with their incompetence. We thought they knew everything. Now, it dawns on us that they know absolutely nothing, especially about the real world. They are demanding, insensitive and have no compassion for our social needs. We can hardly wait for the day we're on our own.

From then on, every emotion a young adult feels towards a parent seems so transient and volatile. For years, they vacillate between like and dislike, love and hate. What sets most adult children off is that they believe they are the resident experts on parenting, while the pair that they are living with are completely ignorant on the subject matter. How easy it is to judge. Of course there are many times when a parent can become irrational, unpredictable or worse, completely unavailable. But, I've got a news flash for you. Parents, underneath all their stuff, are imperfect human beings. Although children would hope that they are their parent's primary focus in life, they are not their sole concern. To add insult to injury, as children mature and become more independent, parents also spread their wings. Parents, as humans, have other needs that must be met, other than parenting every minute of the day. They have careers, relationships, friendships, hobbies, health concerns and more.

We all expect our parents to be perfect and if they can't be perfect, at least be present. When I had my first child, I thought my mother would want to move in. She didn't. Then I assumed that she'd want to see the baby every day. But, she didn't. It took me some time to realize that my mother is not my child's mother. She is the grandmother and has the luxury of visiting whenever it suits her. I'm not upset with my mother, but rather with myself, for having unrealistic expectations. By the time I had my second child, I was living in another city. Whenever my mother can see my children, she does. If that's good enough for her, then it's good enough for me. When I'm a grandmother I will understand how my children feel and still visit when I can.

If you are not a parent, then you can't possibly understand the emotional, physical and financial demands. When there is a lot going on, it becomes difficult to manage everything well. Remember, twenty or more years ago, the literature on parenting skills was not as plentiful and accessible. Even today, many parents remain uninformed. As a result, when a person is under duress, it is their parenting role that takes a back seat and the children suffer. I know this is unfair.

If it sounds as though I am defending parents who have made mistakes, it's because I am. However, it's not their error that I'm defending, but their ignorance, their ineptness and their priorities (or lack of) as parents. I want you to understand that at the time, your imperfect parent was not able to handle all their responsibilities effectively and yes, made bad choices.

Here's another news flash. You will make bad choices, too — if you haven't done so already. You might not make the same bad choices as your parents did, because you know how it feels. You might be more educated and have a better approach. But, you will make mistakes and when you do, I want you to remember what you've read today. The truth is, there is no art in being perfect. Practice being human and that will be your greatest accomplishment.

Marlene, 41 years old
I never really had a relationship with my father. When I needed to talk to someone, I went to my mother. He wasn't even around most of the time. He was either working or sleeping. Even when he was around, he would barely speak to me and when he did, it was always critical. No matter how well I did something, it was never good enough.

I've had two failed marriages. One was to a man who was a workaholic, like my father. The other was to a man who was extremely sociable, unlike my father. I'm attracted to strong men, which is how I view my father. I don't like to be the leader in a relationship. I want someone to protect me and take care of me.

In the last ten years, I have seen such tremendous changes in my father. In hindsight, I can say that my father really didn't know how to be a dad. Even though his way of showing love was by buying me everything that I wanted and anything that he could afford. But, he was doing the best he could. Despite any bad memories, I know my father really cared for me. He just couldn't show it. I understand that now.

Choices

23

It's not what's happening to you now or what has happened to you in your past that determines who you become. Rather, it is your decisions about what to focus on, what things mean to you and what your going to do about them that will deterime your ultimate destiny.

— Anthony Robbins

One of the greatest commodities available to North Americans today would have to be our wealth of choices. Every waking day we are absolutely inundated with multiple choices, meaningless choices and inconsequential, monotonous choices. We choose what to wear, what to eat, which errands to do, whose needs to meet and all within the first hour. The range and magnitude of human choice is phenomenal and often, overwhelming. Thankfully, most are effortless and mundane. However, occasionally we are confronted with a choice that is actually novel, one that forces us to stop and think before we act upon it. Schools, careers, health issues, religious beliefs, relationships, friendships are just a few of the significant, life-changing decisions that we must make throughout our lives. What process does our mind work through to get us to the point of a final decision?

Making choices depends on two factors: the type of person you are and the context of that decision. Take a moment to think about your style. Are you a cautious and methodical thinker or more of a carefree and spontaneous nature? Depending on your present age, you might have started out as one type and then changed over the years. Teenagers and young adults can take an awfully long time to make a choice. Biological clocks aren't ticking, creditors aren't phoning, bosses aren't demand-ing and babies aren't challenging, for the majority. Time is on their side.

As we mature, the bombardment of choices compounded by internal and external pressures taxes our time availability. We make hasty decisions based on social expectations, personal needs and past experiences. Then, when we are confronted with a major problem, we look back on that choice and realize we might have made the wrong one. We are face to face with the discomforting revelation of how very little thought was put into that choice. How we wish, at that instant, that we can go back and rethink that decision, to reselect an alternative, to redefine the outcome.

However, not all choices need to be scrutinized. The context of any decision can assist you in determining whether it should be expedited or not. A complex decision of the heart should take more time than a simple decision of the stomach. Choices that affect your future need more deliberation than those that affect the quality of your evening entertainment.

You can see how personal style and context can facilitate or complicate the process. However, there are less obvious variables, rooted in our memory banks and buried in our subconscious that influence one of our most significant, life changing decisions; choosing to fall in love.

These individuals whom we elect to spend our time with help to define who we are and how we feel about ourselves. Think back to some of your best and worst relationships. Remember how you felt about yourself at that point in your life? Which came first, the person or your state of mind that drew you to him?

The truth is that we attract people who reflect our self-perceptions. And (unless you've already done extensive internal housekeeping), your self-perceptions are a compilation of your past relationships. I'll say this in another way. Your experiences in previous relationships contribute to the formation of your character. In turn, your character attracts certain types of people. This might explain why you keep repeating the same patterns, either in the personality of the men you select or the types of relationships you create.

SHARI R. JONAS

Your past will always resemble your future unless you change how you see yourself, how you feel about yourself, your expectations, your wants and your needs.

This is why it is imperative that at the end of every relationship you do your personal growth homework. Ask yourself what lessons you've learned and how you can benefit from the experience. Review what type of individual would best suit your personality and how you wish to share your life. Perhaps you have already done this and after only a handful of experiences, you have found love and contentment.

However, if you continue to struggle with relationships by repeating poor choices then you must re-examine your very first relationship — between you and your father. The impact of his absence or presence has managed to reverberate throughout every one of your positive and negative relationship choices. Don't fool yourself in believing that you've escaped the emotional impact of being abused, abandoned, neglected or ignored by the one man who should have never let you down.

The study in this book and the stories I have collected support this notion. Before you make one more challenging choice and commit your heart and soul, body and mind to someone less deserving, take some time. You have work to do and by now, you should know what that is.

If I can change anything in my life, I would change some, but not all of my choices. However, I know that spiritually speaking, I am the person I have become because of those choices. They are, in fact, my choices. I made them therefore I own them. I am not the victim of my circumstances, but the creator of my life, which instills in me an empowering sense of responsibility, even for the worst of my mistakes. Sure, I can blame another person, another relationship, another dimension for the choices that I made. But, again, I made them and at times, that's a hard pill to swallow.

I can honestly say that I have often chosen the more difficult path for myself and that I didn't always think things through before I made my final choice. Those of you who have conducted your lives in the same manner know who you are. We are more spontaneous and more passionate than the average individual. So, when we make a choice, all too often it is quick, emotional and filled with righteous convictions. No one can convince us otherwise, once we made up our minds. We are so sure that when we finally make that serious, life-altering choice that it is the best one. But, the method behind our madness is so subjectively ingrained in our past that we can't distinguish how we came to the decision in the first place. How many times have you asked yourself, "What was I thinking?" There are others, still, that might answer that question by saying that they had no choice at all. They did what they did because someone made them, or they believe society imposed it upon them. As if there was this invisible gun pointed to their head and they had to follow the path assigned to them. I don't buy it.

My life has been spent reviewing and rethinking many of my choices in order to learn from them. If you think hard enough, deep enough and long enough, you will come to realize that many of the paths that you have walked on to get you where you are today, were self-directed and self-selected.

Choices, in essence become our life-lessons. Whether they are the right ones or the wrong ones, we are here to learn from them. I would imagine that cautious and systematic people make fewer mistakes because they take the necessary time and effort to make better choices. However, some may argue that they also have much less exciting lives. Change is exciting, it is refreshing, but it can also be painful, detrimental and the spill over onto other peoples' lives that didn't deserve to suffer is often unavoidable.

Yet, the greatest pain of all is the growing pain. In the long run, it is also the most satisfying. Imagine how the caterpillar feels wrapped up in that cocoon for so long? Yes, it is sleeping, as most of us are when we are consumed with our lives. When the transformed caterpillar awakens and works its way out, it finds it self free, at last. Free to open its wings and take to the air. Need I say that the caterpillar has become a beautiful butterfly? There is something incredibly therapeutic in self- realization and transformation. Once we learn from our past, then we, too, can evolve, awaken, be free and let our spirits soar.

SHARI R. JONAS

No matter how old or young you are, every day is a beginning. Although we cannot change what has passed, we can:

Re-examine ... our memories,
Reconnect ... with our inner child,
Adjust ... our self-perceptions,
Shift ... some paradigms,
Reflect ... upon our choices, and
Transform ... our experiences into lessons

Your life is a journey — you are the traveller. Wherever you go, you carry all your experiences in the knapsack on your back. Whenever you meet someone or face a new challenge, you reach to your past for assistance and guidance. But, if all you carry is sadness, anger, insecurity and mistrust, your future will be nothing more than the past you have left behind. Open your satchel, turn it upside down and empty the contents in its entirety. Review your life, remember the people who have impacted it, retain the experiences you've benefited from and leave all other nonsense behind. You can grieve if you want to. You can confront it if you need to. But, you absolutely cannot take it with you on your journey any longer.

May you choose your path wisely, from this day forward.

The brightest future will always be based on
a forgotten past
You can't go well in life until you let go of your past
failures and heartaches.
When you were born, you were crying and everyone
around you was smiling.
Live your life so that when you die, you are the one
who is smiling
and everyone around you is crying.

— Author Unknown

Epilogue

My Dear Shari,

I was so thrilled to receive a copy of your manuscript FatherEffects. *As a Licensed Marriage and Family Therapist I was especially excited to know that someone was addressing the father/daughter relationships.*

Over the years I have worn many hats, however, they typically had one thing in common — victimization. I have presented many work-shops and seminars to Law Enforcement, Judges, Schools, Military, Medical Professionals and Mental Health Professionals and have testified often as an expert witness in criminal and family courts. I have been fortunate to work with victims of crimes as well as the perpetrators of crimes. I am currently the Clinical Director of the South Texas Offender Programs (STOP Programs) in San Antonio, Texas where I work daily as a psychotherapist with rapists, child molesters and other violent offenders and their family members.

Some of the most important work comes from the understanding of how we have been parented, but unfortunately, not much has been written regarding the special effects of the father as a parent particularly where the daughters are concerned. Your work shines a light on a much needed area of information. I believe that it will often be referenced by therapists for bibliotherapy with their clients.

For me personally, the book had me reflect on my own father/daughter issues and it helped me realize that, although my father was an alcoholic and I suffered because of it, as an adult I was able to attain the special relationship that I yearned for before he died. But not without much confrontation, intervention and fear of abandonment, and lasting effects! More importantly, in reading your book I was immediately transported to a place and time involving a client that I worked with for several years, and felt moved to immediately write her story to cherish the memory of her. I have sent the story to you and hope you will be as moved by Becky as I was. Thank you again for lighting the way for many!

Martha

Martha M. Moses, MA, LMFT, RSOTP

Marriage and Family Therapist, Private Practice, San Antonio, Texas; Sexual Trauma Therapist, Private Practice, San Antonio, Texas; Sexual Trauma Therapist, In-Patient Psychiatric Care, San Antonio, Texas Special Investigator Child Protective Services, Sexual Abuse Unit, San Antonio, Texas; Executive Director Rape Crisis Center, San Antonio, Texas; Public Speaker Child Abuse Network, San Antonio, Texas; Ritual Abuse Task Force, AACOG; San Antonio, Texas; Registered Sex Offender Treatment Provider, San Antonio, Texas; Expert Witness

The Ultimate Adverse Father Effect

In Memory of Rebecca

The room was filled with weeping women during a support group, one by one sharing their personal experience of rape. There was a light tap on the door and she walked in, eyes swollen almost shut, random bruises from head to toe, hair unkempt and baggy clothes. She sat quietly in the corner as the other women softly welcomed her. Tears dripped onto her folded hands as her head bowed low. Softly she said, "My name is Rebecca. I should be dead. I was only raped, but I survived."

For four years, almost weekly, Rebecca attended the support groups for rape victims and individual counselling with me. Rebecca was not a tiny frail weakling of a woman. In fact, she stood about 5'11", weight proportionate. Many people would find it hard to believe that this woman could have been victimized so traumatically. Becky was highly intelligent, from a well-bred family. Her father worked in the mental health field and her mother was the chairperson for the local mental health association who had two other children besides Becky. One was a schizophrenic son and the other a morbidly obese daughter. Becky was a well-respected Registered Nurse in the Emergency Room.

Her story: Becky had alternately had memories and went into denial about the abuse she suffered from her father emotionally and sexually and the negligence she experienced from her mother. It seems that when Becky was a teen she began having memories of the bad things her father would do to her when she was as young as three years old. Becky's recollection was that her mother was often a patient in the mental ward of hospitals.

Becky referred to herself as the chosen one because her father wanted to spend so much time alone with her. Over time Becky shared memories of the sexual abuse that she endured, the times that she cried out for help and the times she was never believed. Her mother and father referred her to as a liar. According to her parents, "everyone knew Becky would do anything for attention." No help was given.

In her early teens, Becky began experimenting with drugs and alcohol and hanging out with the misfits. She became sexually promiscuous, ultimately resorting to prostitution. Throughout all of this time, Becky would take breaks from the life, renew her passion for her faith and say her daily rosary and pray to God; not to help her, but to help her parents come to a sense of reality. She would ask in her prayers for them to take responsibility, express regret and remorse for the pain they visited upon her. Becky often related that this was all she ever needed to hear and "I love you". But they didn't come through. Ultimately, Becky ended up with a ritualistic satanic organization that brutally used mind control, sexually assaulted her repeatedly and kept her engaged in the use of heroin. At one point, she overheard conversations about the people taking her to the Caribbean and selling her as a sex slave. She finally escaped and went into a rehab for teens and got clean. With support from community help and good Samaritans, Becky entered a nursing program and became a registered nurse. Still no support or help came from her parents. Her father proclaimed that as long as she insisted on telling lies about him, there would be no assistance and instructed her mother to stay away from her.

On several occasions, while working as a nurse, Becky would fall off the wagon, but each time would reach out for help from A.A. [Alcoholics Anonymous] and N.A. [Narcotics Anonymous]. Or friends. Unfortunately, a "friend" turned out to be a drug dealer and before long Becky was not only working as a nurse in the ER but also prostituting for this friend.

When Becky decide one more time to clean up her act and refused to prostitute herself any longer, this friend and a cohort repeatedly raped and beat her — apparently they thought they had killed her and drove to a field and dumped her body. Becky, always the survivor, became conscious and was able to crawl to a highway for rescue. She was taken to the ER at the hospital where she worked, but no one could identify her. Almost every bone in her face had been broken.

And so we meet, at the support group for rape survivors. Over the weeks Becky's story unfolded in group and therapy sessions. She began

SHARI R. JONAS

to heal outwardly and her beautiful spirit came to the surface. What an amazing woman! Becky returned to work at the hospital, had a makeover, bought new clothes and was thriving until the day (months later) she came into her therapy session, sat down and began to sob. Becky had just received the results of an HIV test — she had tested positive for the virus. Having been actively using drugs and prostituting, Becky regularly took the HIV test and was always relieved each time it showed negative. However, Becky had not taken a test since the rape because she was so intent on getting her life back together. Right or wrong the ultimate conclusion was that the men that assaulted her had infected her. We often processed her feelings about the status of her health, what it meant to her career, the brutalizing of her body and soul. However, when Becky shed tears it was from the yearning to be held by her father and protected by him. Becky so wanted to have him in her life. Seldom did she speak of the need for her mother.

On a day Becky when came in looking particularly confident, she sat down to begin her therapy session, took a deep breath and said, "I want a meeting with my father and I want it to be here, in a session."

We discussed the pros and cons from every angle. (I was very reluctant to facilitate this meeting, however, Becky was determined). The final question was, "What do you want to gain from this meeting?"

Becky replied, "I want Dad to listen to me with his heart and soul and tell me that I am not crazy, that he did do bad things to me. I want him to tell me that he was wrong and take responsibility for his actions. But most of all, I just want him to say, I love you."

A tall distinguished, silver haired gentlemen walked into the room reached out a hand and introduced himself to me. He turned to his daughter who is sitting on the sofa looking like a small child (she is 32 years old) nodded his head and a takes a chair across the room. Becky immediately begins to shed silent tears and Father rolls his eyes and says, "So what are you into now?"

Becky mops her tears away and sits up tall, looks at her father and says, "I want to tell you about things that I remember and ask you questions for clarity — that is all that I want." Mr. Father coldly nods his head. Becky begins with the first memory from childhood and stops at the end of each memory thereafter asking for validation. Mr. Father never nods or shakes his head, but keeps his cold stare right on her face. Becky forges on, recalling memories of horrid abuse. I have never before or since heard anyone open herself so, laying all of her vulnerabilities out without protection.

When she finally spent all of her words and feelings, her father rises from his chair and said very succinctly to her, "Everyone knows that you are crazy, that is why you have been in therapy all of your life. Don't ever darken my doorstep again as long as you live; you are no longer a daughter of mine." Mr. Father did a military about face and walked out of the door. (Please recall that Mr. Father is in the mental health field, mother is chairperson of the mental health association.)

Becky sat quietly staring at her hands, the tears gone. She responded finally by saying, "I guess I will go to plan B."

"Plan B?" I asked.

"I'm a nurse," she said softly, "I know exactly how much potassium it will take to stop my heart."

"So plan B is to kill yourself, why?"

"Because then he will have to feel something and I hope it is guilt."

Being the gentle, ever-loving therapist, I said, "You have lost your mind if you think the person that I just met will feel guilty over your death. Yes, he will feel something, but it will be more in the order of relief. Becky your best game plan is to live and thrive and to succeed so that he will have to look over his shoulder at every turn throughout his life, never knowing when you will show up at his doorstep."

Out of a traumatic and solemn moment, this face with an angelic smile looks up at me and says, "I am a good and loving person, and I have survived!" Becky did survive and thrive and succeed. Although she could no long work as a nurse due to her health, she became a paralegal and worked as an advocate for victims of crime. She moved to another location and surrounded herself with healthy friends and coworkers and wrote to me often of her new found happiness and God's light that constantly shone in her life.

If only that was the end of the story.

SHARI R. JONAS

On Easter Sunday, the year 2000, I was sitting in church and noted that the Mass for that Sunday was in memory of Becky. She'd died the previous year of AIDS. As I turned to offer a prayer of peace to the person sitting behind me my hand took hold of a very sad, meek-looking woman.

Becky's mother looked into my eyes and tears fell, no words were spoken.

. . . and there was no father.

Innocence Lost

With one motion,
With one word,
You took the one thing
That makes a young girl
It wasn't my life
Or my identity
It was the innocence
I held inside
To you it was only a game
Yet, I deal with it every day
I wish to be normal
Like everyone else
But because of you
I have suffered in hell
You think you can win
But that isn't true
Because every time I choose to live
I have defeated you

— Anonymous

A Word From
the Author

Many people asked me how I chose *FatherEffects* as a title for this book — it wasn't an easy task. I wanted an informative title that would generate curiosity and interest, much the same way one would ask the questions, "What are the side effects to that medication? Tell me about the special effects in the movie? Are there any after effects from drinking too much coffee? How were the visual effects of the concert last night?" The definition of "effects" is really what solidified it's appropriate use in the title. "A change or result caused by something or someone, an overall impression." That is exactly what our fathers and our relationship with our fathers have left us with, an impression. That impression has, to a large degree, defined who we are and has contributed to many of our significant life choices. *FatherEffects* examines a father's impression upon his daughter's world. It's that simple. Or is it?

I would love to hear from you about how this book has affected your life. Please share with me any stories or suggestions you might have. You may contact me at *fathereffects@hotmail.com.*

Workbook and Audiocassette

SOON TO BE RELEASED:

The *FatherEffects* Workbook
An Interactive Guide to Healing and Personal Growth

A step-by-step interactive workbook filled with self-help exercises
and solution-focused techniques that will assist you
in your personal transformation.

The *FatherEffects* Audiocassette

A relaxing alternative to reading, narrated by the author herself.

NOTES

NOTES